ALSO BY JOHN ASHBERY

POETRY
Some Trees
The Tennis Court Oath
Rivers and Mountains
The Double Dream of Spring
Three Poems
The Vermont Notebook
Self-Portrait in a Convex Mirror
Houseboat Days
As We Know
Shadow Train
A Wave
Selected Poems
April Galleons
Flow Chart
Hotel Lautréamont
And the Stars Were Shining
Can You Hear, Bird
Wakefulness
The Mooring of Starting Out
Girls on the Run

FICTION
A Nest of Ninnies
(with James Schuyler)

PLAYS
Three Plays

CRITICISM
Reported Sightings: Art Chronicles 1957–1987

YOUR NAME HERE

YOUR NAME HERE

POEMS BY

JOHN ASHBERY

FARRAR, STRAUS AND GIROUX • NEW YORK

Farrar, Straus and Giroux
19 Union Square West, New York 10003

Distributed in Canada by Douglas & McIntyre Ltd.
Printed in the United States of America
First published in 2000 by Farrar, Straus and Giroux
First paperback edition, 2001

Library of Congress Cataloging-in-Publication Data
Ashbery, John.
    Your name here : poems / by John Ashbery.
      p.   cm.
    ISBN 0-374-52783-0 (pbk.)
    I. Title.

  PS3501.S475 Y68 2000
  811'.54—dc21

                    00-039330

The author gratefully acknowledges the following publications in which po-
ems in *Your Name Here* first appeared, sometimes in slightly different form:
American Poetry Review, *Café Review*, *Colorado Review*, *Combo*, *Conjunc-
tions*, *Denver Quarterly*, *Fence*, *The Germ*, *Harvard Review*, *The Hat*, *The
Iowa Review*, *The Kenyon Review*, *Kunapipi*, *Lingo*, *The London Review of
Books*, *murmur*, *The New Republic*, *The New Yorker*, *The New York Review of
Books*, *The New York Times*, *The Ohio Review*, *The Paris Review*, *PN Review*,
Stand, *The Times Literary Supplement*, *Verse*, *The World*, and *Birthday Boy:
A Present for Lee Harwood.*

"Frogs and Gospels" was commissioned by the Getty Research Institute for
the History of Art and the Humanities as part of their program *Humanities in
Comparative, Historical Perspective.*

"Who Knows What Constitutes a Life" was first published as a chapbook by
Z Press with artwork by Elizabeth Murray.

Designed by Jonathan D. Lippincott

For Pierre Martory

1920–1998

CONTENTS

This Room   3

If You Said You Would Come with Me   4

A Linnet   5

The Bobinski Brothers   6

Not You Again   7

Terminal   9

Merrily We Live   10

Brand Loyalty   12

Rain in the Soup   14

Bloodfits   15

Implicit Fog   16

Dream Sequence (Untitled)   17

What Is Written   18

Caravaggio and His Followers   19

Industrial Collage   21

Frogs and Gospels   23

Weekend   25

Get Me Rewrite   26

Invasive Procedures   28

Paperwork   30

The History of My Life   31

Toy Symphony   32

Memories of Imperialism   34

Strange Occupations   36

Full Tilt   37

The File on Thelma Jordan   38

Two for the Road   41

Heartache   42

The Fortune Cookie Crumbles   44

Onion Skin   45

Redeemed Area   46

Variations on "La Folia"   48

De Senectute   50

The Gods of Fairness   52

Who Knows What Constitutes a Life   53

Sacred and Profane Dances   54

Here We Go Looby   56

Avenue Mozart   58

Life Is a Dream   59

Vowels   60

Beverly of Graustark   61

The Pearl Fishers   63

They Don't Just Go Away, Either   64

Conventional Wisdom   66

And Again, March Is Almost Here   68

A Descent into the Maelstrom   70

Sonatine Mélancolique   71

Stanzas before Time   73

A Postcard from Pontevedra   74

A Suit   75

Crossroads in the Past   76

The Water Inspector   77

Cinéma Vérité   78

The Old House in the Country   79

Autumn Basement   80

Hang-Up Call   81

Lost Profile   82

How Dangerous   84

Humble Pie   85

More Hocketing   86

Amnesia Goes to the Ball   88

Railroaded   89

Honored Guest   91

Our Leader Is Dreaming   92

Last Legs   93

Lemurs and Pharisees   94

The Underwriters   96

Pale Siblings   97

Nobody Is Going Anywhere   98

Poem on Several Occasions   99

Slumberer   100

Pot Luck   103

Short-Term Memory   105

Vendanges   106

Small City   108

Vintage Masquerade   110

To Good People Who Should Be Going Somewhere Else   111

Another Aardvark   112

Has to Be Somewhere   113

The Don's Bequest   115

Strange Cinema   116

A Star Belched   117

When Pressed   118

The Impure   119

Crowd Conditions   120

Enjoys Watching Foreign Films   121

Fade In   122

Over at the Mutts'   123

Pastilles for the Voyage   124

Of the Light   125

Your Name Here   126

YOUR NAME HERE

THIS ROOM

The room I entered was a dream of this room.
Surely all those feet on the sofa were mine.
The oval portrait
of a dog was me at an early age.
Something shimmers, something is hushed up.

We had macaroni for lunch every day
except Sunday, when a small quail was induced
to be served to us. Why do I tell you these things?
You are not even here.

IF YOU SAID YOU WOULD COME WITH ME

In town it was very urban but in the country cows were covering the hills. The clouds were near and very moist. I was walking along the pavement with Anna, enjoying the scattered scenery. Suddenly a sound like a deep bell came from behind us. We both turned to look. "It's the words you spoke in the past, coming back to haunt you," Anna explained. "They always do, you know."

Indeed I did. Many times this deep bell-like tone had intruded itself on my thoughts, scrambling them at first, then rearranging them in apple-pie order. "Two crows," the voice seemed to say, "were sitting on a sundial in the God-given sunlight. Then one flew away."

"Yes . . . *and then?*" I wanted to ask, but I kept silent. We turned into a courtyard and walked up several flights of stairs to the roof, where a party was in progress. "This is my friend Hans," Anna said by way of introduction. No one paid much attention and several guests moved away to the balustrade to admire the view of orchards and vineyards, approaching their autumn glory. One of the women however came to greet us in a friendly manner. I was wondering if this was a "harvest home," a phrase I had often heard but never understood.

"Welcome to my home . . . well, to our home," the woman said gaily. "As you can see, the grapes are being harvested." It seemed she could read my mind. "They say this year's vintage will be a mediocre one, but the sight is lovely, nonetheless. Don't you agree, Mr. . . . ."

"Hans," I replied curtly. The prospect was indeed a lovely one, but I wanted to leave. Making some excuse I guided Anna by the elbow toward the stairs and we left.

"That wasn't polite of you," she said dryly.

"Honey, I've had enough of people who can read your mind. When I want it done I'll go to a mind reader."

"I happen to be one and I can tell you what you're thinking is false. Listen to what the big bell says: 'We are all strangers on our own turf, in our own time.' You should have paid attention. Now adjustments will have to be made."

A LINNET

It crossed the road so as to avoid having to greet me. "Poor thing but mine own," I said, "without a song the day would never end." Warily the thing approached. I pitied its stupidity so much that huge tears began to well up in my eyes, falling to the hard ground with a plop. "I don't need a welcome like that," it said. "I was ready for you. All the ladybugs and the buzzing flies and the alligators know about you and your tricks. Poor, cheap thing. Go away, and take your song with you."

Night had fallen without my realizing it. Several hours must have passed while I stood there, mulling the grass and possible replies to the hapless creature. A mason still stood at the top of a ladder repairing the tiles in a roof, by the light of the moon. But there was no moon. Yet I could see his armpits, hair gushing from them, and the tricks of the trade with which he was so bent on fixing that wall.

THE BOBINSKI BROTHERS

"Her name is Liz, and I need her in my biz," I hummed wantonly. A band of clouds all slanted in the same direction drifted across the hairline horizon like a tribe of adults and children, all hastening toward some unknown destination. A crisp pounding. Done to your mother what? Are now the . . . And so you understand it, she . . . I. Once you get past the moralizing a new winter twilight creeps into place. And a lot of guys just kind of live through it? Ossified soup, mortised sloop. Woody has the staff to do nothing. You never know what. That's what I think. Like two notes of music we slid apart, far from one another's protective jealousy. The old cat, sunning herself, had no problem with that. Nor did the diaphanous trains of fairies that sagged down from a sky that suggested they had never been anywhere, least of all there. At the time we had a good laugh over it. But it did hurt. It still does. That's what I think, he slapped.

NOT YOU AGAIN

Thought I'd write you this poem. Yes,
I know you don't need it. No,
you don't have to thank me for it. Just
want to kind of get it off my chest
and drop it in the peanut dust.

You came at me and that was something.
I was more than a match for you, you
were a match for me, we undid the clasps
in our shirtings, it was a semblance of all right.

Then the untimely muse got wind of it.
Picked it up, hauled it over there.
The bandy-legged man was watching
all this time. ". . . to have Betty back on board."

Now it's time for love-twenty.
Assume your places on the shuffleboard.
You, Sam, must make a purple prayer
out of origami and stuff it. If you've
puked it's already too late.

I see all behind me small canyons, drifting,
filling up with the space of drifting.
The chair in the attic is up to no good.

Then you took me and held me like I was a child
or a prize. For a moment there I thought I knew you,
but you backed away, wiping your specs, "Oh,
excuse . . ." It's okay,
will come another time

when stupendous seabirds are carilloning out over the Atlantic,
when the charging fire engine adjusts its orange petticoats

after knocking down the old man the girl picks up.
Now it's too late, the books are closed, the salmon
no longer spewing. Just so you know.

TERMINAL

Didn't you get my card?
We none of us, you see, knew we were coming
until the bus was actually pulling out of the terminal.
I gazed a little sadly at the rubber of my shoes'
soles, finding it wanting.

I got kind of frenzied after the waiting
had stopped, but now am cool as a suburban garden
in some lost city. When it came time for my speech
I could think of nothing, of course.
I gave a little talk about the onion—how its flavor
inspires us, its shape informs our architecture.
There were so many other things I wanted to say, too,
but, dandified, I couldn't strut,
couldn't sit down for all the spit and polish.
Now it's your turn to say something about the wall
in the garden. It can be anything.

MERRILY WE LIVE

Sometimes the drums would actually let us play
between beats, and that was nice. Before closing time.
By then the clown's anus
would get all chewed up by the donkey
that hated having a tail pinned on it,
which was perhaps understandable. The three-legged midgets
ran around, they enjoyed hearing us play so much,
and the saxophone had something to say
about all this, but only to itself.

Clusters of pollen blot out the magnolia blossoms this year
and that's about all there is to it. Like I said,
it's pretty much like last year, except for Brooke.
She was determined to get a job in the city. When last heard from
she had found one, playing a sonata of Beethoven's (one
of the easier ones) in the window of a department store
downtown somewhere, and then that closed, the whole city did,
tighter'n a drum. So we have only our trapezoidal reflections
to look at in its blue glass sides, and perhaps admire—
oh, why can't this be some other day? The children all came over
(we thought they were midgets at first) and wanted
to be told stories to, but mostly to be held.
John I think did the right thing by shoveling them under the carpet.

And then there were the loose wickets
after the storm, and that made croquet impossible.
Hailstones the size of medicine balls were rolling down the slope anyway
right toward our doorstep. Most of them melted before they got there, but
    one,
a particularly noxious one, actually got in the house and left its smell,
a smell of violets, in fact, all over the hall carpet,
which didn't cancel one's rage at breaking and entering,
of all crimes the most serious, don't you fear?

I've got to finish this. Father will be after me.
Oh, and did the red rubber balls ever arrive? We could do something
with them, I just have to figure out what.
Today a stoat came to tea
and that was so nice it almost made me cry—
look, the tears in the mirror are still streaming down my face
as if there were no tomorrow. But there is one, I fear,
a nice big one. Well, so long,
and don't touch any breasts, at least until I get there.

BRAND LOYALTY

"Father, you're destroying the collectibles!"

"You are mistaken. I'm enjoying them! The green magenta finish on this one reminds me of the piano shawl in our flat in Harbin—only greener, as though slits of light were coming through its slits."

"At least we have the lilacs."

How he would get a little too creative, God and I both know. He's spent the morning chiding the waterspout, clearly amazed as it drew increasingly closer. "I've had it with natural phenomena. They never know when to draw the line. At least we have some sense, and we're natural phenomena too, for goodness sakes."

I wouldn't let it get to me. On the other hand, the waterspout or whatever you call it *is* getting to us. It touched down, back there, and only a moment ago it was in front of us. I suggest we sidle along the sand.

The deuce you say! On the other hand, if you really think so.

We could offer it tea and cookies, but in a moment it'll be too late for anything but palsied brooding on the tired theme of retribution. Like I said, they build them stronger and stronger until it's encoded in them. They can't help putting their best foot forward, and where does that leave us! After all, a little peace was all we were after.

If only you'd read up on the subject like you said you were going to.

Yes, well we can't alarm our surroundings too much, even as they torture us. That way we'd only slip out of pain and not see the exciting denouement. And what a sweet-tempered morning it was. Put aside our notions of the intrepid, the universe is paying a courtesy call, God has us on hold, and there's not much we can do except spin like dervishes, human tops. Hair climbing upward to a point, a kind of spire, and all I'd done was brush down the sides.

Can we do it that way now?

Not exactly. The village is walking toward us, we are becoming its walls and graffiti-sprayed cement bathrooms, its general store, the tipsy taxi driver. If I told you where we were going it wouldn't be a surprise anymore, and yet it would . . .

Sounds like my friend Casper, the girl said.

RAIN IN THE SOUP

Raindrops fall on the treetops. A rainy day.
Yes, it's that kind of a day. Some human suffering.
A number of malcontents. If Mr. Soup
will stay in his bowl, I'll blow on him.
Elsewhere stockings are being darned.
The darning egg is as big as a house.

All this less-than-great happiness
may be doing good to life somewhere else,
off in the bayou. Maybe. But we see it
from the top, like a triangular dome,
so it looks okay to us.

Unicyclists are out in force,
leading to the Next Interesting Thing
that's sure to be gone by the time you and I get there.
I don't count ivy climbing a chimney,
that's reached the top and is waving around, senselessly.

I'd like to push a raft down the beach,
wade into the water waist-deep, and get on it.
But clearly, nothing in this world was made for me.
It's sixes and sevens, the chimes go out
into the city and accomplish something valid.
I can stand to stand here, standing it, that's all.
Good day Mrs. Smith. Your daughter is as cute as anything.

BLOODFITS

As inevitable as a barking dog, second-hand music
drifts down five flights of stairs and out into the street,
adjusting seams, checking makeup in pocket mirror.

Inside the camera obscura, jovial as ever,
dentists make all the money. I didn't know that then.
Children came out to tell me, in measured tones,
how cheap the seaside is, how the salt air reddens cheeks.

Violently dented by storms, the new silhouettes
last only a few washings.
Put your glasses on and read the label. Hold that bat.
He'd sooner break rank than wind.
He's bought himself a shirt the color of Sam Rayburn Lake,
muddled ocher by stumps and land practices. Picnicking prisoners
never fail to enjoy the musk that drifts off it
in ever-thickening waves,
triggering bloody nostalgia
for a hypotenuse that never was.

IMPLICIT FOG

We began adulating
what we were staring at
too:

I was following the paths in the music.
Might as well have been patting myself dry
under a toadstool.

Winter came on neck and neck
with spring, somehow.
The two got tangled up for reasons
best known to themselves.
By the time it was over
summer had ended

with a quiet, driven day
out under the trees
in folding chairs:
troops ejected from a local bar.

It got lovely and then a little hirsute.

DREAM SEQUENCE (UNTITLED)

Yes, she chopped down a big tree.
We could all breathe easier again.

It wasn't the hole in the landscape
that gladdened us, it was the invitation to the weather
to drop in anytime.

Which it did, in proportion to our not growing interested in it.

After a third mishap we decided
to throw in meaning. No dice.
Our tapestry still kept on reviving itself
athwart the scary shore. You could look into it
and see fog that had been dead for years,
cheerful hellos uttered centuries ago.
Worse, we were going somewhere;
this was no longer the bush leagues, but a cantata
nature had ordered from the celestial caterer,
and now it was being delivered.

There were only a few false notes; these mattered less
than a cat in a cathedral. Suddenly we were all singing
our diaries of vengeance, or fawning thank-you notes, or whatever.
The hotel billed us by the hour
but for some reason the telegraph wires weren't included
in the final reckoning. Too, the water-tower had disappeared
as though deleted by a child's blue eraser.

It was then that the nets of chiming
explained what we had needed to know years ago:
that a step in the wrong direction is the keyhole
to today's busy horizon, like hay, that seems to know where it's moving
    when it's moving.

WHAT IS WRITTEN

What is written on the paper
on the table by the bed? Is there something there
or was that from another last night?

Why is that bird ignoring us,
pausing in mid-flight, to take another direction?
Is it feelings of guilt about the spool
it dropped on the bank of a stream,
into which it eventually rolled? Dark spool,
moving oceanward now—what other fate could have been yours?
You could have lived in a drawer
for many years, imprisoned, a ward of the state. Now you are free
to call the shots pretty much as they come.
Poor, bald thing.

CARAVAGGIO AND HIS FOLLOWERS

You are my most favorite artist. Though I know
very little about your work. Some of your followers I know:
Mattia Preti, who toiled so hard to so little
effect (though it was enough). Luca Giordano, involved
with some of the darkest reds ever painted, and lucent greens,
thought he had discovered the secret of the foxgloves.
But it was too late. They had already disappeared
because they had been planted in some other place.
Someone sent some bread up
along with a flask of wine, to cheer him up,
but the old, old secret of the foxgloves, never
to be divined, won't ever go away.

I say, if you were toting hay up the side of a stack
of it, that might be Italian. Or then again, not.
We have these things in Iowa,
too, and in the untrained reaches of the eyelid
hung out, at evening, over next to nothing. What was it she had said,
back there, at the beginning? "The flowers
of the lady next door are beginning to take flight,
and what will poor Robin do then?" It's true, they were blasting off
every two seconds like missiles from a launching pad, and nobody wept, or
     even cared.
Look out of the window, sometime, though, and you'll see
where the difference has been made. The song of the shrubbery
can't drown out the mystery of what we are made of,
of how we go along, first interested by one thing and then another
until we come to a wide avenue whose median
is crowded with trees whose madly peeling bark is the color of a roan,
perhaps, or an Irish setter. One can wait on the curb for the rest
of one's life, for all anyone cares, or one can cross
when the light changes to green, as in the sapphire folds
of a shot-silk bodice Luca Giordano might have bothered with.
Now it's life. But, as Henny Penny said to Turkey Lurkey, something

is hovering over us, wanting to destroy us, but waiting,
though for what, nobody knows.

In the night of the museum, though, some whisper like stars
when the guards have gone home, talking freely to one another.
"Why did that man stare, and stare? All afternoon it seemed he stared
at me, though he obviously saw nothing. Only a fragment of a vision
of a lost love, next to a pool. I couldn't deal with it
much longer, but luckily I didn't have to. The experience
is ending. The time for standing to one side is near
now, very near."

INDUSTRIAL COLLAGE

We are constantly running checks.
Quantity control is our concern here, you see.
No batch is allowed to leave the premises
without at least a superficial glance along the tops
of the crates. For who knows how much magic
may be imprisoned there?

Likewise, when the product reaches the market
we like to kind of keep an eye on things there too.
Complaints about the magic
have dwindled to a mere trickle in recent years.
Still you never know if some guy's going to get funny
and tamper with the equation, causing
apocalyptic sighs to break out in the streets,
barking dogs, skidding vehicles, and the whole consignment
of ruthless consequences. That is why we keep a team of experts
on hand, always awake, alert for the slightest thread of disorder
on someone's pants. In spring these incidents can double, quadruple,
        even.
Everything wants to be let out of its box come April or May
and we have to test-drive the final result before it's been gummed
into the album dark farces regulate. Someone, then, must be constantly
on duty, as well as a relief contingent, for this starry mass
to continue revolving.

Like an apple on the ground
it looks at you. The neighborhood police were kind,
arrested a miscreant, though he was never brought to trial,
which is normal for this type of event.
Meanwhile spring edges inexorably into summer,
where, paradoxically, there is more activity but less to show for it.
The merry-go-rounds begin turning in the carnivals of August.
Best to leave prison till winter, once the honor system has broken down.
A stalemate could pollute new beginnings.

November tells it best, in a whisper almost,
so that there is surprisingly little letdown,
only this new background, a finer needle to thread.

FROGS AND GOSPELS

How does one interpret, on this late branch, the unexpected?
—James Tate, "The Horseshoe"

A chance balloon drew these settlers nigh.
It was the year of green honey that sprouts
between the toes of the seated god. "None
can explain it further." No explanations,
not from me.

I sat in the bakery, rumpled, unshaved,
pondering a theorem. What you said the hotel was.
Someone else's towel approached me in the laundry.
"Ouch was what I said." This has been more than I know of,
brimming with indifference, some American in Europe.

He let me off at the corner of some strange country.
The signs were in English. No one cared if
you knew the rubbish was filth.
He carried me from the room in which people were sitting.
They always think they know better, even as they confess
their ignorance blindly, to the first stranger they know.
I see, it's a market garden, or was
some seasons ago. In this dark stubble I abide.

A messenger came with tidings. I'm sorry,
I've had enough tidings.
Giddy with surprise, he crawled upward
toward where I was toasting myself.
A male muse I suppose. I've listened to that
before, too. All I want is to be let out
to travel on the gravel. You still don't
get it, this is a seat. All right, I want my seat,
I said.

That's no easy manner. The blond moon came untied,
drifted through blue-black wisps
of a woodpile somewhere. Must I follow her too?

Must I follow her too?

Whatever it says you must do.
You had calm days in store, now they have come undone.
Worries stretch before you into the distance.
Perhaps distance is what you had,
once, and must now drink. Only forty years ago
early skyscrapers arched their backs, waiting to be fed.
And still the feeling comes on.

WEEKEND

Swan filets and straw wine,
an emphatic look to the driveway
whose golf clubs are scattered feelingly.

You can undress and sit down
on the corduroy doormat blowing
and when the Weird Sisters come calling
pretend to be talking to yourself.

Trouble is they don't come calling,
suffering as they do from terminal agoraphobia.
A frog juts from a pinecone.

My goodness was that you back there?
You sure know
how to give a feller a good scare.
I'd thought it was just bats
dripping tar on the heads of the guests and the footmen.
You see so little live action in this town
and then everybody wants to cooperate
or celebrate, sort of. I can do that too.
Always. Have a good time.
Something might come out in group therapy:
your velvet soul as I just realized it.
Please come back. I liked you so much.

Thistles, dandelions, what do we care?

GET ME REWRITE

The
ghoulish
resonance
of
a
cello
resonates in a neighbor's cabana.

What do I know of this?
I
am
sitting
on a pile of dirt in a neighbor's back yard.
Was there something else to do?

Long ago we crept for candy
through the neighbor's gutter
but found only candy wrappers
of an unknown species: "Sycamores,"
"Chocolate Spit," "Slate-Gray Fluids,"
"Anamorphic Portraits of Old Goriot."

The way a piece of candy seems to flutter
in the prismatic light above a clothesline, stops,
removes all its clothes.
There was a bucket
of water
to wash in,
fingerposts pointing the way to the next phenomenon:
sugar falling gently on strawberries, snow on a pile of red eggs.

None of us was really satisfied,
but none of us wanted to go away, either.
The shadows of an industrial park loomed below us,

the brass sky above.
"Get off your duff," Reuel commanded.
(He was our commander.)
"You are like the poet Lenz, who ran from house to forest
to rosy firmament and back
and nobody ever saw his legs move."

Ah,
it is good
to be back
in the muck.

INVASIVE PROCEDURES

> I flee from those who are gifted with understanding, fearing that all
> their great and illuminating invasions of my being still won't satisfy
> me.   —Robert Walser, "The One of Fairy Tales"

Massachusetts rests its feet
in Rhode Island,
as crows rest in cowslips
and cows slip in crowshit.

I may have been called upon to write
a poem different from this one.
OK, let's go. I want to please everybody
and this is my song:

In Beethoven Street I handed you a melon.
Round and pronged it was, and full of secret juice.
You, in turn, handed me over to the police
who thought (correctly) that I was the spy
they had been looking for these past seven months.

They led me down to their station, you need to know,
where they questioned me for days on end.
But my answers were always questions, and so they let me go,
exasperated by their inability to answer.
I was a free man!
I walked up Rilke Street
chattering a little hymn to myself.
It went something like this:

"Beware the monsters, but take care
that you are not yourself one.
Time is kind to them

and will take care of you,
asleep on your grandmother's couch, sipping cherry juice."

How did the pigs get through the window screens at night?
By morning it was all over.
I had never sung to you, you never coaxed me to
from your balcony, and all trains run into night
that collects them like paper streamers, and lays them in a drawer.

Unable to leave the sight of you
I draw little crow's feet in my notebook, in the sunlight
that comes at the end of a sudden day of tears
waiting to be reconciled to the fascinating madness of the dark.

My mistress' hands are nothing like these,
collecting silken cords for a day when the wet wind plunges
through colossal apertures.

Suddenly I was out of hope. I crawled out on the ledge.
The air there was frank and pure,
not like the frayed December night.

PAPERWORK

Waste time on these riddles?
Because what would I lecture on then?
The master that comes after, after all,
brushes them aside or burns them.
Am I therefore not very strong?
Will my arch be built, strung along the sand
within sight of olive trees? No,
I am cut of plainer cloth, but it dazzles me
in the evening by the moonlight.

L'heureuse, they called her.
Day after day she gazed at the blue gazing globe
in her sunlit garden, saying nothing.
Noticing this, the old stump said nothing too.
Finally it couldn't stand it any longer:
"Can't you *be* something? You have the required manners
and your dress is a shifting of pea-green shot with sea-foam."

I know I shall one day come to the reason
for manners and intercourse with persons.
Therefore I launch my hat on this peg.
Here, there are two of us. Take two.

Turning and turning in the demented sky,
the sugar-mill gushes forth poems and plainer twists.
It can't account for the roses in our furnace.
A motherly chimp leads us away
to a table overflowing with silverware and crystal,
crystal smudgepots so the old man could see through tears:

He is the one you ought to have invited.

THE HISTORY OF MY LIFE

Once upon a time there were two brothers.
Then there was only one: myself.

I grew up fast, before learning to drive,
even. There was I: a stinking adult.

I thought of developing interests
someone might take an interest in. No soap.

I became very weepy for what had seemed
like the pleasant early years. As I aged

increasingly, I also grew more charitable
with regard to my thoughts and ideas,

thinking them at least as good as the next man's.
Then a great devouring cloud

came and loitered on the horizon, drinking
it up, for what seemed like months or years.

TOY SYMPHONY

Palms and fiery plants populate the glorious levels of the unrecogniz-
able mountains.   —Valéry, *Alphabet*

Out on the terrace the projector had begun
making a shuttling sound like that of land crabs.
On Thursdays, Miss Marple burped, picking up her knitting
again, it's always Boston Blackie or the Saint—
the one who was a detective
who came from far across the sea
to rescue the likes of you and me
from a horde of ill-favored seducers.

Well, let's get on with it
since we must. Work, it's true
suctions off the joy. Autumn's density moves down
though no one in his right mind would wish for spring—
winter's match is enough. The widening spaces
between the days.

I sip the sap of fools.
Another time I found some pretty rags
in the downtown district. They'd make nice slipcovers,
my wife thought, if they could be cleaned up.
I don't hold with that.
Why not leave everything exposed, out in the cold
till the next great drought of this century?
I say it mills me down,

and everything is hand selected here: the cheeses,
oranges wrapped in pale blue tissue paper
with the oak-leaf pattern, letting their tint through
as it was meant to be, not according to the calculations

of some wounded genius, before he limped off
to the woods.

The stair of autumn is to climb
backward perhaps, into a cab.

MEMORIES OF IMPERIALISM

Dewey took Manila
and soon after invented the decimal system
that keeps libraries from collapsing even unto this day.
A lot of mothers immediately started naming their male offspring
    "Dewey,"
which made him queasy. He was already having second thoughts about
    imperialism.
In his dreams he saw library books with milky numbers
on their spines floating in Manila Bay.
Soon even words like "vanilla" or "mantilla" would cause him to vomit.
The sight of a manila envelope precipitated him
into his study, where all day, with the blinds drawn,
he would press fingers against temples, muttering "What have I done?"
all the while. Then, gradually, he began feeling a bit better.
The world hadn't ended. He'd go for walks in his old neighborhood,
marveling at the changes there, or at the lack of them. "If one is
to go down in history, it is better to do so for two things
rather than one," he would stammer, none too meaningfully.

One day his wife took him aside
in her boudoir, pulling the black lace mantilla from her head
and across her bare breasts until his head was entangled in it.
"Honey, what am I supposed to say?" "Say nothing, you big boob.
Just be glad you got away with it and are famous." "Speaking of
boobs . . . " "Now you're getting the idea. Go file those books
on those shelves over there. Come back only when you're finished."

To this day schoolchildren wonder about his latter career
as a happy pedant, always nice with children, thoughtful
toward their parents. He wore a gray ceramic suit
walking his dog, a "bouledogue," he would point out.
People would peer at him from behind shutters, watchfully,
hoping no new calamities would break out, or indeed

that nothing more would happen, ever, that history had ended.
Yet it hadn't, as the admiral himself
would have been the first to acknowledge.

STRANGE OCCUPATIONS

Once after school, hobbling from place to place,
I remember you liked the dry kind of cookies
with only a little sugar to flavor them.

I remember that you liked Wheatena.
You were the only person I knew who did.
Don't you remember how we used to fish for kelp?
Got to the town with the relaxed, suburban name,
remembering how trees were green there,
greener than a sudden embarrassed lawn in April.
How we would like to live there,
and not in a different life, either. We sweltered
along in our union suits, past signs marked "Answer"
and "Repent," and tried both, and other things.

Then—surprise! Velvet daylight
came along to back us up, providing the courage
that was always ours, had we but
known how to access it downstairs.

We used to crawl to so many events together: a symphony
of hogs in a lilac tree, and other, possibly more splendid,
things until the eyelid withdrew.

Now I can sample your shorts.
So much more is there for us now—
runnels that threaten to drown the indifferent one
who sticks his toe in them.
Much, much more light.

To whose office shall we go tomorrow?
I'd like to hear the new recording of clavier
variations. Oh, help us someone!
Put out the night and the fire, whose backdraft
is even now humming her old song of antipathies.

FULL TILT

Disturbing news emanates from the wind tunnel:
He's gone, who never lacked for champions,
killed by daylight saving time, or a terrible syllabus accident.

The dead leaves, maple or aspen, are a sign of life.
Let's leave things as they are,
drying in the sun, soaking up the sweetness
that's in everything.

This is what taking chances was all about, and look where it's led us!
To the root, it seems of human misery.
Misery, get up, get down. Your hair is a mess
and your dress a fright. Yet your curdled armpits
speak to us. Sometimes it's better to have nothing to say
when you are telling about what happened today.
It was so much, after all, that morbid agenda.

Now, why not investigate the way
all this can end up being pretty? Not just the whore
who waits on the corner till the last sliver of taxi is gone,
to be repackaged next night in a department store window
so you can pretend you bought it? I'm up here, Louise,
we're all up here, waiting for you to step up to home plate
and bat us a cool one. Oh, but
I was supposed to be in the station an hour ago.
That's the way it gets illustrated:
the four of you in Cincinnati, waving across the plain
to us, the lemon in hot pursuit, leading to student unrest.

We don't have to worry about that now—
tomorrow or the day after will be just as good.
The fraternity has already waited an eternity. Only coaxing the stars
out could produce the fruit you need to have in your stocking or shorts.

Then this scene too faded away like a fable.

THE FILE ON THELMA JORDAN

Coldly, we put away the cabin flatware.
Tomorrow, a transport strike. Damaged vacations will result.
What the fuck, we're already in one and have somehow
got to make it what with the living, you know,
the sport and recreation around. Pious reflexes too.
So now about the apple? You know, what about it?
Vague chintzes all around, her hair caught in the door.

It seemed time when the bus came for Jacques in Vienna
that the other Boston terriers would be having their day too,
but no such luck—the sapphire eyes of one, confused,
were just about it. You could go away, too.

A poseur held up a scroll which, predictably, cascaded to the floor.
Something about an annual charity bazaar. We'd forgotten
it again, in the garden, this year. Why must things emerge
before you've finished wisecracking about them. What
does it all mean? In what rut were you born? I've got to
fix the baby's things. I'm on my way to the garret. Don't come.
I assure you everything is under control. It's of no importance.
Stop it. I said it's not that important. What's not important?
What couldn't be under the blue sails dripping
as they develop, develop their theories about us,
haunting the ether with memories of clay? We haven't a stitch
to wear. Rumson's is having a sale. I thought I'd
got out of that one. Oh no? A car is having its way with her,
carrying us down to the beach, against our will, as if by magic.
The chorus of foresters raises their muskets in a silent
gesture of solidarity with the departed. There, I thought
I'd finish this story before making another mistake and now it's
happening. Oh, dear! Grace, fetch some ketchup, will you?
Now, there it's all better. As I was saying . . .

Strangers salute you in the street,
brave marquis of many years. What are thy wishes?
A shore dinner would be nice, perhaps on the boat launch
where we could feel for mussels afterwards. I like that,
reminds me of an encyclopedia I once read in an afternoon.
Oh yes, well, there were always a lot of stories
about how you played and who won. Nobody set much
store by any of them, but now you two men are like bricks
in a chimney, nobody is going to separate you or carry you off
or stand by you much longer, once the office closes.
Did it? It's five o'clock and there are no roses . . .

I thought I'd followed that street to the end
but it was only the end of the beginning, the rest was transparent
and needle-pure. "Best have a look at it." The sun goes down
with a plop in these parts, like an egg falling on a counter,
and who is there to count the endless waterfowl, water ouzels,
beavers with otters on their backs? I'll take that chessboard.
I mean I want it back now. But the tanks
rolling in the city hinted at another scenario,
another worst-case one. Listen to the pretty snowflakes.
Oh, I love you so much in such a little time.
It seems a shame we have to go on living. I mean,
we could get more loving into it. I'm not quitting.
I mean, I am but I'm not a quitter.
Whoever said you were? Climb up that cello and try to get some rest.
In the morning I've got to see the accountant.

So it goes, in the old country as well as in the new.
Pelicans startle us, then some reason for living gapes
in the wall of a building that once housed a bookstore
and is now for sale. The unlikeliest bidders come and go,
pandering to the lower orders shall I say
and the unguents who made all this possible. Let's give them a hand . . .

Hey, you don't think there's any more
over the horizon? I'm not sure I could stand it if there was,
I mean their faces. Oh, they'll all be home for Christmas
sometime, I'm sure. Why don't you take a little trip
to an aching village? You look tired. Are you OK?
It was just my brother calling from Wichita. He says the downtown's on
      fire.
Well if I was you I wouldn't go there.
No, I have no intention of doing so.
Now, about those missing "fish" cards, did your nanny
take it into her head to "hide" them in her workbasket
or did Sheila abscond with them?

I'm not saying the boys isn't responsible.

It was two of them to one of us in one box.
After the team finished cheering the fridge opened by itself, violently,
as one thinks of spring tempests tearing into trees,
mindless of viaducts below. People are wearing hound's-tooth more.
That's one way you can sense the change
in the average person's deportment. I'm trying to unpack
these worthless drachmas so as to get the twins off to school,
Hey, some of those could turn out to be valuable.
Says who, and besides it's raining in the next street and all around town.
Finny creatures lurch by. We must try frying the endive
next time. In the meantime my noggin will sport a red golfing cap
in case there's anyone around to see, which at this hour is unlikely,
I admit, but I intend to have the old niblicks at the ready
just in case, and it's sure foul out. Don't jolt that.
It pertains to me. It's a stuffed raven given to my great-grandfather by
Edgar Allan Poe himself. Said he was finished with it. It had cost him a
      poem,
though, a great one. Want to hear . . .

Did you want it plain or frosted? (Plain vanilla or busted?)

I bet you've been writing again. She reached under her skirt. Why don't you let a person see it? Naw, it's no good. Just some chilblains that got lodged in my fingertips. Who said so? I'll tell you if it's any good or not, if you'll stop ___ ing it with your hand.

Highlar te's sake—
651-695

Merrian d forgotten that it was noon, the hour when the ravens emerge from
651-642-(r beside the huge clock face and march around it, then back inside howers. Oh, where were you going to say let's perform it?

Rice Str
651-558 ght it was evident from my liquor finish steel.

Riverv ght, you can certainly have your cocktail, it's my shake, my fair shake.
651-2 t-colored hydrangeas fell out of the pitcher onto the patio. Darned if meone doesn't like it this way and always knows it's going to happen like his when it does. But let me read to you from my peaceful new story:

R
(

"Then the cinnamon tigers arose and there was peace for maybe a quarter of a century. But you know how things always turn out. The dust bowl slid in through the French doors. Maria? it said. Would you mind just coming over here and standing for a moment. Take my place. It'll only be for a minute. I must go see how the lemmings are doing. And that is how she soiled herself and brought eternal night upon our shy little country."

HEARTACHE

Sometimes a dangerous slice-of-life
like stepping off a board-game
into a frantic lagoon

drags the truth from the bathroom, where it has been hiding.
"Do whatever you like to improve the situation,
and—good luck," it added, like a barber adding an extra plop of lather

to a stupefied customer's face. "When they let you out
I'll be waiting for you." It had been that way ever since a girl with braids
teased him about getting too short. Yeah, and I'll bet they have

places for people like you too. Trouble is, I don't know of any.
The years whirled quickly by, an upward spiral
toward what ghastly ascendency? He didn't know. He cried.

One November the police chief came calling.
He had secretly been collecting all the bright kids
in the universe, popping them into a big bag

which he lugged home with him. No one was too sure what happened
after that. The kids were past caring; they had the run
of the house after all. Was it so much better outside?

Snow lashed the windowpanes as though punishing them
for having the property of being seen through. The little town
grew quieter. No one missed the kids. They had been too bright

for that to happen. Night sprang out of the dense cold
like an infuriated ocelot with her cub that someone had been trying
to steal, or so it pretended. The frightened townspeople sped away.

There was no longer any room on the sidewalk
for anything but "v's" drawn in pink chalk, the way a child
draws a seagull. Down at the tavern the neon glowed a comforting

red. "All beer on tap," it said, and
"Booths for Ladies."

THE FORTUNE COOKIE CRUMBLES

You have a kind and gentle nature. Not overly
challenged more than once. The "small things" matter
once you've replaced the dish on the shelf
and moved very convincingly toward the door.
"Just dying for attention," you've been around
the block yourself a few times, paid the bills
and furniture. You were a tulip
in some past life, it says here. You have "two lips,"
as winy and luscious as a Chevy
in your dad's garage.

On a sorry note, your correspondent
notes that you have a tendency to fly off to Europe
at the slightest provocation. Must mean you're getting old,
or "devoid of charm" is maybe what it says.

It is likely that a viable present can be brokered.
Your past is all used up now, anyway.

The lilies love you more than ever
now, it seems. I love you too, but my brow
is furrowed.

I mean, what am I going to tell my shoe?

ONION SKIN

In the end it was their tales of warring stampedes
that finished us off. We could not go them one better
and they knew it, and put our head on a stamp.

"Then I should have some pain, too?"

REDEEMED AREA

Do you know where you live? Probably.
Abner is getting too old to drive but won't admit it.
The other day he got in his car to go buy some cough drops
of a kind they don't make anymore. And the drugstore
has been incorporated into a mall about seven miles away
with only about half the stores rented. There are three
other malls within a four-mile area. All the houses
are owned by the same guy, who's been renting
them out to college students for years, so they are virtually uninhabitable.
A smell of vitriol and socks pervades the area
like an open sewer in a souk. Anyway the cough drops
(a new brand) tasted pretty good—like catnip
or an orange slice that has lain on a girl's behind.

That's the electrician calling now—
nobody else would call before 7 A.M. Now we'll have some
electricity in the place. I'll start by plugging in
the Christmas tree lights. They were what made the whole thing
go up in sparks the last time. Next, the light
by the dictionary stand, so I can look some words up.
Then probably the toaster. A nice slice

of toast would really hit the spot now. I'm afraid it's all over
between us, though. Make nice, like you really cared,
I'll change my chemise, and we can dance around the room
like demented dogs, eager for a handout or they don't
know what. Gradually, everything will return to normal, I
promise you that. There'll be things for you to write about
in your diary, a fur coat for me, a lavish shoe tree for that other.

Make that two slices. I can see you only through a vegetal murk
not unlike coral, if it were semi-liquid, or a transparent milkshake.
I have adjusted the lamp,
morning's at seven,

the tarnish has fallen from the metallic embroidery, the walls have fallen,
the country's pulse is racing. Parents are weeping,
the schools have closed.

All the fuss has put me in a good mood,
O great sun.

VARIATIONS ON "LA FOLIA"

Now another one who said it is gone,
killing all the wonderful suspense, desired or not.
Shut the window. It's chilly in here.
Yes, I know it's only open a crack.

It's "all moon and no stars" again,
and I cast no shadow.
It's not a good thing.
There aren't that many seats.

I remember when Clement Attlee was world premier.
There was more austerity then but less things to get done.
The amniotic valley still holds memories of those
kids who have sway, some blue-violet,
some only an outline. It was what he meant by austerity,
I think. There was a man named Silhouette once,
renowned for his stinginess.

As I think about it the more it gets lighter and brighter.
I had asked for it monogrammed.
A hurricane blasted the triple-mud sundae
into the room where I like to write sometimes in the afternoons.
There was no dealing with the gangsters then.
They all had disappeared.

My dog, green pussy, came along with my bowl of grape-nuts.
I let out an unaccustomed howl
yet no hoosegow gaped.
I was wholly on my own.

Hollyhocks strangled the windmill's blades
till it stopped to ask for more, for directions
where it was going, which obviously was nowhere.
Cormorants clove the air. Men had poured oil

on their eggs to prevent them from hatching
so as not to reduce the fish population,
though the fish had never asked for that. Far from
it. They believed in the equality of the species,
that a pesky bird was worth no more and no less than a dumb fish.
Man, again, is the interloper here. He takes whatever he chooses
from the dish life holds out, then acts surprised
a century or two later when the world has spun out of control,
and wakes up scratching his head, wondering what happened.

We should all be so lucky as to get hit by the meteor
of an idea once in our lives. It would save a lot of hand-wringing
and bells tolling in the undersea cathedral,
a noise to drive one mad, past the brink of human decency.
Please don't tell me it all adds up in the end.
I'm sick of that one.

DE SENECTUTE

Whatever charms is alien.
Throw it back in the water, makes no difference.
I was amazed at your absence, child,

from the chapel's round window.
You forgot, you see.
And me, sometimes.

There is true worth strapped away in there.
Fifty is young today. So's eighty. Depends
on which side you're looking at it from.

And she leans toward purple colas,
returns with salt on her tunic's hem.
Too crazed to cry. In which she resembles

all of us. I'm not going to the benefit.
I hate charity. But it's the greatest
of the three. Can't help it, I'm an old boa

constrictor. I feel about life much as you do:
as a diary from many years ago. We thought we'd caught
something in March, some kind of flu,

but it lasted even until now,
though no one remembers it. You will,
upon opening your garage door, stumble

on some unpleasant evidence of the neighbor's dog's
recent passage. Is there anything you can do?
No. Later on in spring, when the robins

are nesting, something will splat on your car's windshield
or windscreen. Again, it profits not
to go looking for causes and effects

in a froth of rage whipped up
by someone else. August with its cooling showers
from the hose invites us to take a breather.

Yes, a breather is what we've longed for,
can get no closer to
than the rain barrel, its surface of dust and

fruitflies. Well, back to work
again. It is the one thing that won't be
denied that won't save us. Pensively, the watch crystal's

warning us to be off, ere another hour strikes.
Oh, I love you so much in such a little time
it seems a shame to have to go on living.

Yet another hour protrudes. The imps
have all become children. Well, wish them away.
The pyramid's gravitas

will never manifest itself with them around.
The wolf took up a broom and swept the walk
up to the front door, and seemed to

want to be petted for its efforts.
The hell with that. The empty corral
is on the point of coming into being, a "perfect"

circle, brand new as you please.
Somebody, someone in authority, said it was all a joke,
so we packed up and went home that day.

THE GODS OF FAIRNESS

The failure to see God is not a problem
God has a problem with. Sure, he could see us
if he had a hankering to do so, but that's
not the point. The point is his concern
for us and for biscuits. For the loaf
of bread that turns in the night sky over Stockholm.

Not there, over *there*. And I yelled them
what I had told them before. The affair is no one's business.
The peeing man seemed not to notice either.
We came up the strand with carbuncles
and chessmen fetched from the wreck. Finally the surplus buzz
did notice, and it was fatal to our project.
We just gave up then and there, some of us dying, others walking
wearily but contentedly away. God had had his little joke,
but who was to say it wasn't ours? Nobody, apparently,
which could be why the subject was never raised
in discussion groups in old houses along the harbor,
some of them practically falling into it.
Yet still they chatter a little ruefully: "I know
your grace's preference." There are times
when I even think I can read his mind,
coated with seed-pearls and diamonds.
There they are, for the taking. Take them away.
Deposit them in whatever suburban bank you choose.
Hurry, before he changes his mind—again.

But all they did was lean on their shovels, dreaming
of spring planting, and the marvelous harvests to come.

WHO KNOWS WHAT CONSTITUTES A LIFE

Really? Uncle Pedro is coming
with his entire entourage? They want
to take over the whole top floor?
They say they'll be arriving soon? Day
after tomorrow? Not in a century,
I bet. These things are like dreams
of things that are real. And they really exist
beyond the breezeway, where no man has ever been.

How, then, can we be confident
they are solid and peaceful, like chimeras?
The shit list is long
and extends far back into the last century.
If we admit them *now* . . .

I was just standing on the landing
and a rush of air whooshed by me
on its way to the attic. I caught the scent
of Uncle Pedro's discreet *eau de toilette*
(notes of lily-of-the-valley and wild hickory bark)
but to conclude that I am involved in this,
or that any of it is my affair, is, well,
downright dour. I am off on my own again,
will return in an hour
to see if the house has burned down
or the calf given birth to calflets.

SACRED AND PROFANE DANCES

If all you want is kittens,
come back later. At dusk. No later.
The kittens will be in by then.

"What if I said I want no kittens,
just a big fat you?" The Motorway City,
Leeds, has more of them, more varieties.
And I said I just couldn't. Mime the dialogue
any faster. They're taking rollcall now.

With all the spontaneity of a sarabande
he wakes up, showers, puts on a tie,
jumps in his Dodge and drives to work.
Here there are other, secret choices.
He cannot look at them. He must needs leave this place,
office, whatever. The beavers look at him endangered
from their saw-palmetto-shrouded photomural.
No matter, he's driving to this special house.

Word gets out. He makes a U-turn
and is soon speeding along a numbered highway
out in the country somewhere. "How did it get so itchy?
So late?" They bind him to the trash
and escort him up the ramp, to the sacrificial slab.
Oh? Well, if that's the way things work out,
more power to 'em. Being is only a way of being.
When in doubt, fast forward, I always say.

Now that it's Christmas and Mother
there must be an explanation for the shadows,
the gaps in the grass of the downs
over there. "Ssh. Don't think."

And I was all for a descent into a churn
in my diving helmet. Funny the way things work out.

I said, it's funny the way things work out.

HERE WE GO LOOBY

Where is that tricycle, man?
You know I set much store by it
since there is nothing else in the world right now.

Here is the church and here is the steeple
and the vast hill that recedes under them
down to the squirrel's nest. He has to have one,

you know. She wrote letters and crushed them
under her pillow. Years later they turned up
in the mill race floating quietly, secretively,
near the shore. I'll

get up and get one. No,
you won't. This is strictly the governor's business,
who held hands with Miles Standish, or Priscilla—
a tectonic unrest made less awkward
by the distribution of the braille mail and disposing
of table scraps. Sometimes one gets caught in a pail,
"in pailed." And the doily scissors scallop your tootsies
as though primitive man had lived this way all along,
just waiting for you to show up and be astonished.

In truth sir you are a jaybird.
But just come with us and everything will work out fine,
I'm sure. Oh no you don't, that's the way you got me the last time,
you bastard and I let them punish me for it. Gentlemen,
we've a problem here. On the one hand I don't want to appear too harsh,
but his lackadaisicalness is truly unconscionable—I—I
just don't have a word for it.

Now I want the flower girls to appear stage left.
The peacocks and our mother will take care of everything else.
I am unperched, dispossessed, and this is the helpful truth of it,

the holy harp I keep harping on.
If they had wanted it another way they would have arranged it

that way. It would be cruel to dwell much longer in their collective
    memory
and I'm ready for a shower. Oh, just one thing—
did that guy ever tell you where my tricycle is, or the light switch?
It was all a drawing on canvas, you see. This way no one gets hurt,
and a few of us learn something.

AVENUE MOZART

Some of these houses are startlingly old.
Other, newer ones seem old too.
Only when a line of trees ends in something
Does it resemble the model of progress glimpsed once
in a bottle as a boy. Our references have all aged a little
as we were looking at them, not noticing.
Now there's something perverse in every yellow leaf,
every cat loafing, even the stick leaning against the door.
I'd like to get out of these clothes . . . "Later."

And a full moon of oxymorons swings up over the ridgepoles
with their chimneys. It's light enough to read by.
But nobody feels like reading now.

LIFE IS A DREAM

A talent for self-realization
will get you only as far as the vacant lot
next to the lumber yard, where they have rollcall.
My name begins with an A,
so is one of the first to be read off.
I am wondering where to stand—could that group of three
or four others be the beginning of the line?

Before I have the chance to find out, a rodent-like
man pushes at my shoulders. "It's *that* way," he hisses.
"Didn't they teach you *anything* at school? That a photograph
of *anything* can be real, or maybe not? The corner of the stove,
a cloud of midges at dusk-time."

I know I'll have a chance to learn more
later on. Waiting is what's called for, meanwhile.
It's true that life can be anything, but certain things
definitely aren't it. This gloved hand,
for instance, that glides
so securely into mine, as though it intends to stay.

VOWELS

Instant insufficiency edged eerily over our oasis.
Under us, awed angry Airedales adjusted.
The octet closes with a signing-on in shipyards.
Through naked fingers of the rain
Easter week, and during the winter the valleys
are like yeast. This much I divined, walking,
then turned my back on the mighty fragment of yesterday.

Everything was at peace with everybody. A dark stone glistened.

BEVERLY OF GRAUSTARK

It's wind, it's sleeting.
It's real adventure. It hasn't happened yet.

It's time to break for lunch—
half a bean sandwich. Yours isn't here yet,
you asked for black bread on bacon.

The perp is becoming abusive,
and I would like a chiller, wind
in my pants, my long taffeta gown,
to take me anywhere from any place
before this insane excursion is finished. Please—
the seamstress is inside down below.

The president of Slavonia is on the wire:
We'll have to go ahead with the order for flatbed trucks
now stretching far into the offended distance.
Stop! Some other way may be found—
That's what you think, sister.

The day extracts, in a loosely confining way,
what these pills signified,
and what they were supposed to absorb before your seconds arrived
and now it's too late to include the meeting.
It would only baffle the establishment.

Yes but what I am hearing is from plazas of wailing
tilting back into the bland exposure of it,
the idle secret. It was again a lunch of sandwiches,
but truth will perforate. As sadly as I'm
in your line of vision, Venice is closed,
another browser sidles in
through a snow of ecstatic fleas,
what my alma mater is all about I think I once said.

Photographs of members enjoin us through the back seat
on a spring day once; green grass and toilets
spooled on a little anticipation.

"Nelly"—that's all I needed and we're off again, down foul alleys
ending in meticulous squares, and none of us knew the outcome yet.
We could see the blue ice-slick clear through the Turkish uniform,
and the bowling alleys ended out in the garden as is right
and proper.

Poor Beverly—they never gave her (him?) a chance
to prove herself in the journals of the East End
before being summoned to that rocky principality
from which no bulletins ever issue—only brickbats
and the occasional red herring press release: "Collapsed
felt underdrawers are invading the season, counsels
Léopoldine from Phalsbourg, but don't
dare disguise those shoulder pads yet. Instead, why not
think rotting horseflesh this year? Some beaux even prefer it
to the spritzed violets so common underfoot
these days of walking back to the starting gate
where everything began, inconceivably it seems, in light—"
a fiery bazaar no one needs to talk too much about anymore
till the next in the round of visits happens.

It's incredible though how few latent oblivions have been canceled—
we're back on track at least as far as
late returns are concerned. Most of them are in.
A few hotel ghosts wander stiffly, wondering if catarrh
can ever be cathartic, and if there's any afterlife, and if so,
whether it's near as the next room, or the closet even,
which might just be preferable to daytime's sloping agendas,
the roof at night, the rent, and the violet pallor flooding us now always.

THE PEARL FISHERS

And he would say, "You ought to write him and thank him for it," and I'd
say, "Yes, I'm going to when I have the time." Of course I had intended
to, but the project aged. It was slightly too dry. I'll begin again, I'll
thank him. And so I did, in my own way. I forgot him and his seven
    journeys
to success. We became as one—a stilt. A single stilt isn't of much use,
and that's how I thanked him—by reminding him from time to time,
as the salt ball rolled toward the glacier.

It melted and did not. Wait, you can't get up. There's A.1. sauce

on her slipcover. Informality be damned, he said. Whenever I come here I
like to take two lumps instead of three. Unfortunately you can't have either,
we're out of everything I said. The sun smiled wanly on the Cimmerian
    landscape,
which stirred. It seemed as if it was at last about to take an interest

in rubber goods,
piles of filth,
gossamer undies,
potted hyacinths,
stumps no tree would own up to,
casinos rattling till three in the morning.

I'm sorry, Mrs. Swan-toe,
we meant not to disturb and then this waterfall
rushed over the island, as I'm sure you noticed. By the time it had passed
fully, except for the occasional unavoidable runnel,
no one could remember how to count.

It was a Royal Accident.
You can't rely on those,
they always win.

THEY DON'T JUST GO AWAY, EITHER

In Scandinavia, where snow falls frequently
in winter, then lies around for quite some time,
lucky cousins were living in a time-vault of sorts.
No purchase on the ground floor, but through a funnel-shaped drain
one could catch glimpses, every so often, of the peach-colored
firmament. It's so terrific! It's purer than you think,
too, not that that need unduly concern us.

Father sat in his living room
off the main parlor, working at his table. We never knew
exactly what he did. We kids would amuse ourselves
with games like Authors and Old Maid, until Mamma abruptly
withdrew the lamp, and we all sat shivering in the dark for a while.
Soon it was time to go to bed. We groped our way up
non-existent flights of stairs to the attic funnel.
Everything is so peaceful in here I can dream of more kinds
of things at once. But what if the dreams were prophetic?
Stumbling down an alley, screaming, forehead bathed in blood
or ossified like an old tree root that can barely speak, and when it can,
says things like: "Do you know your horse is on fire?"

Many winters were passed in this way.
I cannot say I feel any wiser for it.
Instead my brain feels like a face freshly shaved
by the barber. I rub it with satisfaction,
giving him a good tip on the way out.
More fanciful patterns await us further along
in our destiny, I tell him, and he agrees; anything
to be rid of me and on to the next customer.
Outside, in the street, a length of silk unspools beautifully,
rejoicing in its doom.

Father, I can go no farther, the lamp blinds me
and the man behind me keeps whispering things in my ear

I'd prefer not to be able to understand . . .
Yet you must, my child, for the sake of the cousins
and the rabbit who await us in the dooryard.

CONVENTIONAL WISDOM

Although I have known you for a long time
it seems as though we hardly know each other at all.
It was as a rehearsal for coming to be in time
that leaves are aslant. Take another look
for the cookie hoarded in armpits up till now,
the pointed stare.

When the satchel came undone I was running around
the corner please, sure as a clock's breath
in the allées, digging. Heaven sent this pinprick.
It was another time to be riding around in.
Alright I said I can take care of myself.
Then depth spun its wheels. I was sliding on gravel somewhere.
Take a look around you for your personal belongings
before getting on this bus. Not one but three old ladies came along.
The flustered caddy spoke for the local cesspool contractor when he said
man the trailer I thought I belonged here but what
the hey, said in wartime the beets were too much spinach.
Now I can unclog you be patient.
A girl in the apse wondered why the cymbals
were drained of vowels in these perplexing times.
Have you ever read Rimbaud's Les Voyelles No I haven't I said.
It's too much like the class room in here. Now if we replaced the air
with cobwebs wouldn't they all march in correctly
to the triangle's tune? Sure, the major is bound to be pissed off
but all that counts is our air conditioner. In a jiffy
the dock was rehabbed. The colonel grabbed Mavis and Iris.
It's dumb overhead. I know this but please,
let's resolve our differences in gentlemanly fashion. What'll it
be, swords or soldier beetles. My is there a difference?
Mayhap only in dreams where you bottle it and sell it.

And the can fell off the radiator.
Althea's glazed look came true. It was deep blue in the palaces

of revolt. Something extraordinary was happening
all the time. The due date kept flashing past

the diamond slot in fishnet pumps and a shadow,
the shadow of the lunge on the bridge,
of monsters congealing above the town,
and of a lost slip with my name on it in the cradle of the ages.

AND AGAIN, MARCH IS ALMOST HERE

If I were a tree you'd say
I was lost by a highway.
Death overflows the ditches
in which life confined it
and will be that way for some time.

I saw the alchemist drown
in his turquoise at seven
and elsewhere saw the less spiritual side.
God, how it gets me down.

Then furtively a bailiff came
as though to take my measurements
for a new suit. "Here, I don't need this . . .
brine." I was cluttered for the day.

A Mrs. came out of her house
being as I was on the road to say
look for the heather that is father
to the salt hay down the road.

I guess I only confused
my eager willingness to understand
just about anything that was offered.
Alas, it wasn't much.

There were few requests for employment
and those seemed old and pallid
as though faxed by a squid one day last March.
Now, a year has gone by. Not quite

a year though, as I
was going to say.
They offered me Bluebeard.
So much that was unacceptable

that day and all the forests to come.
Though bathed in sleep and aromatic
persons, other stimuli come to the aid
of the hairs of one's neck:

a lad on a bicycle, once,
beautiful as the crescent moon;
enjoyable as a book in a long set of books
who asks you this secret again.

A DESCENT INTO THE MAELSTROM

Hell no, the creators weren't anguished,
just determined to keep you dangling
above the maelstrom a few more seconds.
Then it was as if everything that was going to happen
had. Here, walk into my living room,
put on these sandals, you must be tired.
You've come a long way since the evening news
put a half-nelson on both of us. Here,
drink this sugared tea.

It was as though my childhood were beginning again,
with bills to pay, defective homework to be done,
and the rain getting in, wanting to play, it seemed,
like a cat. A great big cat loves me, I guess.
I was down in the swamp tuning my viola,
and naturally everybody comes by then to ask you for a favor,
or, more rarely, to offer to do one for you.
I guess they think nobody ever goes outdoors.
Me, I can't understand it. It's the dicey ones
can't, the car waxers, the dictators. Then say hello to him
by all means, though I guarantee he won't know what you're saying.

SONATINE MÉLANCOLIQUE

Then I walked on a ways.
It became apparent that the journey (for
such it was) was far from unavoidable.
A twig skewered my sock
and I looked up at the oak tree's strapless trunk,
hoping to escape from what seemed a parable,
from which escape is never possible.

I know *that*. But there is still time for surprises
like the time you looked at me and smiled
just as the sledge was dragging us past a bunker
scented with antique urine. In short

it is here that I shall found a colony
and call it God.

The wasps that night had never been loonier,
making reading impossible. I put down my volume
of *Little Dorrit*, and gnats flung themselves even closer
with propositions. "Hey, how'd you like to be rid of that guy
and us too? All you need do is push a button
and a mandarin somewhere on the other side of the world
will stagger for a moment, seeing his life transpire
before him: that first bowl of gruel, graduation day
at mandarin school, and later on doubts and remorse,
a flummoxed present that seeps into the past,
making a whole life seem regrettable." No,
I cannot condone your offer, the thick answer is for later.
Meanwhile I shall try to pacify my eyeballs
with the mist leaking from the ceiling.

That proved sufficient, caressing the knocker,
a goblin's face, that drew us back a hundred years
even as it gazed at us in surprise, speechless

as a field of daisies, to a time when we too were out of step
and the whole sentient world offered to bathe us—
pale bluster, flubbing today again and again.

STANZAS BEFORE TIME

Quietly as if it could be
otherwise, the ocean turns
and slinks back into her panties.

Reefs must know something of this,
and all the incurious red fish
that float ditsily in schools,

wondering which school is best.
I'd take you for a drive
in my flivver, Miss Ocean, honest, if I could.

A POSTCARD FROM PONTEVEDRA

Just how I feel
I feel today.

The witch stirred the soup
with a magic spoon.

She said, "We can make this happen.
We can never make this happen?"

Excuse me? I was waking up
at the Maison Duck you see.

People are walking past me,
faster and faster—it seems they are running toward something.

Call me old-fashioned. No, don't,
on second thought. We'll call an ambulance

instead. I was waking up with this humming in my ears—
sound of the sea, of a basket of nettles.

It's O.K. to ride, to not go along. I'm not sure
where Pontevedra is. If I was I'd have to ask myself

so many other questions, ones you never
taste in the brightness of your day,

though they answer me
like the risen sea.

A SUIT

The audience was scattered forever, and the story left untold.

—from the film *Careful*, by Guy Maddin

Maybe it only looks bedraggled.
Let's take it up to the fifth floor and see.
One can look quite far in that light, into the corners
of experiences we never knew we had, that is to say most of them.

But the city is new. The new apartment building, now vacant,
circles like a moth that as yet has no idea
it's trapped in a spider's web, that the indelible
will soon come to pass. For a few moments now
we can drink tea and talk of the famous doll collection
in the museum of a small European spa.
Shadows on the tent alert us: Breathing isn't going to be as easy
as we'd thought once. Mr. Cheeseworth is always so right
in his calculations, yet when one comes to believe him, where is he?

It has been a life of qualification and delay.
Yet we knew we were on the right track; something surged in us,
telling us otherwise, that we'd arrive too early at the airport
or something about the drips on the taxi in the dusk.
We doctored it all up,
and I think I have an explanation for the manna
that falls softly as pollen, and tastes like coconut or some other
unaccountable sherbet. It seems clothes never do fit.

Yes, I could have told you that some time ago.

CROSSROADS IN THE PAST

That night the wind stirred in the forsythia bushes,
but it was a wrong one, blowing in the wrong direction.
"That's silly. How can there be a wrong direction?
'It bloweth where it listeth,' as you know, just as we do
when we make love or do something else there are no rules for."

I tell you, something went wrong there a while back.
Just don't ask me what it was. Pretend I've dropped the subject.
No, now you've got me interested, I want to know
exactly what seems wrong to you, how something could

seem wrong to you. In what way do things get to be wrong?
I'm sitting here dialing my cellphone
with one hand, digging at some obscure pebbles with my shovel
with the other. And then something like braids will stand out,

on horsehair cushions. That armchair is really too lugubrious.
We've got to change all the furniture, fumigate the house,
talk our relationship back to its beginnings. Say, you know
that's probably what's wrong—the beginnings concept, I mean.
I aver there are no beginnings, though there were perhaps some
sometime. We'd stopped, to look at the poster the movie theater

had placed freestanding on the sidewalk. The lobby cards
drew us in. It was afternoon, we found ourselves
sitting at the end of a row in the balcony; the theater was unexpectedly
crowded. That was the day we first realized we didn't fully
know our names, yours or mine, and we left quietly
amid the gray snow falling. Twilight had already set in.

THE WATER INSPECTOR

Scramble the "Believer" buttons. Silence the chickens. We have more important things, like intelligence. We say so many cruel things in a lifetime, and yet. In a whorehouse, young, I obfuscated. Destiny was this and that, no it was *about* this and that. Do you see what I'm saying? Nobody needs the whole truth.

Even so we exact repetition. The beat goes on. Terribly surprised about the report, about your father's death, but these things happen. Often the dead are found next day, alive but shaken, wondering what it was that happened to them, trembling beneath a cellar door. And we too wonder what happens when the sky as we know it cracks in two. Beetle voices serenade us. The earth and its fountains can't do enough for us, yet we remember, shaken too, like in the old days.

We were reading and there came a knock at the door. The water inspector, we thought, and of course no one was there. Stung, and stung again. So we proceed, always on course, always begging the stars to tell us what happened, whether we were clean really, were we on course. Always the silence says yes, you can go home now, round up your playmates, head for the nearest wooded area if you think that will help.

I was once surprised but lay and brooded, my life at my back now, my discourse like weeds far out on a lake. It must have come to me, it always does, part of my profound business.

I think in the think tank, always elegant in my thinking, far away. Far from what I consider. Once it was all grace in the lifting. Awkward, yes, and not a little disconcerting.

CINÉMA VÉRITÉ

Be kind to your web-footed friends, I murmur to myself half anxiously, hurrying to the movies. After all, a duck *may* be somebody's uncle. Or niece. I am lost. I ask directions of a horse-faced policeman who gives no satisfying reply. Or is it? "Somewhere up there . . . You'll be sure to find it," he offers. I'd like to wipe the smug expression off his cheeks. Or is it a kindly and beatific smile? I continue along what I think is my way and come to a grassy riviera, a few rusted hotels browsing among smug new ones. A large red and yellow plastic sign says, "Cinema."

Those rocks have a basalt look about them. I was here before once. I can tell by the way the breeze scurries by, patting my cheek as it does so. O solemn breeze! You are the one thing I wanted to have happen to me, the only thing that matters in this concrete canyon of years, so why can't I get close to you? Already you have made off with the chickens I was taking to the cinema, planning to have them for dinner later. Now I shall go hungry, for you and for them, telling my adventures to anyone who will listen, outside on the slippery alabaster stairs. Or in the roomful of people?

THE OLD HOUSE IN THE COUNTRY

The walls are whitish. Is it cold enough in here? No,
it's the statuary I came to see. And the gizzards, you wanted the gizzards
too? No, it was buzzards
I'd mentioned in my letter of introduction, which you seem to have lost,
but I was reminded too of ancient blizzards
that used to infest these parts. Ah, but gizzards
breed sapience, there can be no other way.
Allow me to pass in front of you
while I keep you waiting in the draft that is colder
than the room it besmirches.

Now we can see eye to eye, and it is a good thing.
I would not have thought it easy to set off the smoke alarms
had we been closer together.

"*Now* is the time for escape, you fool."

Don't you see it another way
back in the ridges that bore you, that nature knitted for you?
I don't know, but something keeps getting in the way
of our orderly patrolling of these rooms.
I suppose it's that I want to go back, really . . .

And so you shall, on the 7:19. Meanwhile examine this bronze.
I'll get Biddy to set out the tea-things
and that will save us some time.

AUTUMN BASEMENT

I lost my notes, or they were useless. Luckily
I had scribbled down this number on the baggage claim.
The countess remarked, and with reason, that they
only hold you up if you appear to have been dipped
in aspic. Alas, such was my case. Two hedgerows

further and I'd have made it. Now a rag chairperson gives me the
    runaround,
thinks we met once on a breakwater—
I say, a glass of tea would clash with the silence
of the conundrums, keeping your clatter from me,
safe from me, that is. Would you—er—mind?

So each gets immobilized with a diamond stickpin
under the barrel vault that was invented at just about that time—
notice its groin—and there'll be capers with rabbit for supper
again. I don't know how much longer I can stand August,
though September was always his favorite month, and here
it comes with a packet of unscented breeze.
Yet it always seems that salt should be savory,
the embers more at ease. The moving picture lights, and having lit
perfects a new way out of the shimmering maze. Pity we can't
lingo here forever, but no one lives forever,
or so I've been told.

HANG-UP CALL

Preposterous. That was the word she used,
one much admired for its overtones of thrift and conviction.
I let her go where she wanted with it.
After all, *I* wasn't there to hear it,
looking somewhat dazed amid the regatta
and its ships—or are they one and the same?
Every restful person pauses here
to ask me a question. I have a few ideas
but they wouldn't interest you by a country mile,
not by a million of 'em. Some day I'll have to release my antidote
for disappearing ink (hint: it contains mummy)
and a few other of the brilliant ideas
I've managed to put aside in this old life of mine,
but until that day comes I see no reason to get excited—
hey, wait, *you* were the one who was asking *me*!
That's antenna-dust sparkling on the shoulder
of your silk patchwork bolero. I wasn't even going
to be part of this, remember? I never signed on.
All I remember is press gangs working the bars in Bristol
and waking up on a heap of moldy straw
with a lump the size of a duck's egg on my cranium
and a taste of iodine in my mouth.

But it wasn't me we were going to discuss, remember?
As far as I'm concerned there have been no arguments;
ergo, I have never lost or won any.
Now give me my pants and money and let me go
back and join the others. They're crying, you know.

LOST PROFILE

I had a voice once,
braid falling over the front
of my forehead-house and down the sides.
No need for cream separators here
someone said. My guide took it as a compliment.
Anyway, we got here. Somehow. Now the question

is losing relevance since water is everywhere,
like a transparent mine. I lost my voice a long time ago.
Voices of children ripple endlessly,
endorsing new products. The lizard-god explodes.

The lady on the next bar-stool
but one didn't seem to understand
you when you spoke of "old dark house" movies—
she thought there must be an old dark house somewhere
and you wanted to take her there.
Still, my arrival flabbergasted her,
since it suggested you had no such thing in mind,
at least for the present.

And today I am a mad Chinese monk
chasing after his temple. Which way did it go?
Around that corner of bushes? Or was there ever
a temple? It seemed more and more likely
that it was a figment of your imagination, a figment
perhaps like many another, only a little more underripe.
Undeterred, I chase it in the madness of the gathering dusk
that crashes into ponds, trees, scared bridges.
It had to have been back here somewhere—

As if the air were pure lightning
and the earth, its consort, benevolent thunder,
I can stand and finally breathe.

Light shrinks from the edges of my fingernails
and armpits. This is a page that got bound in the diary
by mistake. It seems we were so happy once, just for a minute.
Then the sky got clouded, no one was happy or unhappy
forever, and the dream of the oppressor had come true.

HOW DANGEROUS

Like a summer kangaroo, each of us is a part
of the sun in its tumbling commotion. Like us
it made no move to right things, basking where the spent stream
trickled into the painted grotto.

Yes, and the snow-covered steppe, part of the same opera,
stretched into dimness, awaiting the tenor's aria
of hopelessness. Yet no shadow fell across any of it.
It might have been real. Perhaps it was. Stranger tales
have been spun by travelers in unreassuring inns
while the last embers collapse one into the other, waking
no riposte. "It was at a garrison in central Tadzhikistan."
And then sort of get used to it, and then not be there.

Each noted with pleasure that the other had aged,
realizing as well that new scenery would have to be sent for
and transported thousands of miles over narrow-gauge railroads—

a fountain in a park, a comforting school interior,
a happy hospital—and that, yes, it would be worth waiting for.

HUMBLE PIE

Various flavors recite us.
Meanwhile the inevitable Casper David Friedrich painting
of a ship pointing somehow upward has slipped in like fog,
surrounding us with vowels of regret
for the things we did not do
rising like a great shout above the barrel.

I was going to say I kissed you once
when you were asleep, and that you took no notice.

Since that day I have been as a traveler
who scurries to and fro among nettles, never sure
of where he wants to end up, a Wandering Jew
with attitude.

All this time the sun had its eye on us
as it was going down. Finally, when it hit the horizon,
it had something to say. Something like pick up your two weeks' salary
on your way out
and don't ever let me catch you on *this* planet again.

Fine, but on what token shore
are we to be misted? We all have to end up somewhere together.
Might as well be in last week's parish newsletter
or in the elbows of a nubian concubine.
I mean, we *are* right, somehow right, which is the same
thing only more so. Sticks and tokens
are my hymn to the sun that has gone,
never to return, it seems,
though.

MORE HOCKETING

The fear was that they would not come.
The sea is getting rougher.
There is a different language singing from the wall.
No singing from the wall.

The fear was that they would come.
Here, have one of these.
Have this one. No, have this one.
To have followed an adage
almost from the beginning of life, through
suburban pleats and undergrowth shrugged
off like underwear on a dinner plate.

Then to emerge fast
into where it's taken you:

no more figs, pretzels. Breakfast's
run out of steam.

And the last car has left.
Let those who never denatured another's remark
swim in wit now. Let the curtains fall
where they may. They are only in distress today.

We have further inversions, like father
and his children sewed up for a day.
Like the feathers you enjoy, the mail
you enjoy receiving.

You have successfully undermined the mountain that threatens us.
Now, panthers prowl the streets.

I took a streetcar that turned into a bus toward the end.
God rewarded me with chirping yellow fuzzballs.

I intended a sonnet that turned out a letter
when Rose crossed the road with her nose
and her father is doing better.

I always like it when somebody explodes out of a bush
to congratulate me on my recent success
for which I'm only partly responsible:
The siblings helped, they prevented it from melting
so high among the Alps you'd have thought it stayed frozen
always. Apparently not. Now we might have a riot
if everybody would calm down for a second.

A shadow-person conducted me along a road
to a little house where I was fed and absconded
with the clock on the wall. I told them I was mortal
and they seemed to let me go. Yet no one heard me.
I was as dust one takes a glove to,
a white one, then tosses in disgust, leaving it lie
in all the trickling creases you absorbed
in childhood, loving it. Two doors went away.

We were alone at last, as they say.
These winters can button you up.
They say Canada geese mate for life, or
till one of them dies, whichever is shorter.

AMNESIA GOES TO THE BALL

In the avuncular waiting rooms they begin handing out the handouts. For some reason my name isn't on the list. But I receive my handout anyway— somebody obviously recognized me and knew I should get one. I open it without much enthusiasm. When was it I last received a manual for regular sex? There isn't much distinction in it, nor does it totally lack distinction. I rearrange my orange suit. Modular sex was what it actually says. This starts me off on a new train of ideas, complete with gambling and smoking lounges. I am not to capitalize on this moment. It is already particularized.

So always going down into new things. It's as though the clouds somehow don't matter—yet look at them! Was anything so enormously real ever explained away before? And who is history anyway? Does it have a bum?

I have to finish this or pretend it isn't written. The Sheriff of Heck is coming over and you know what that means. Ocarina blasts building up the fake festive restiveness, yet you and I know what a gardenia is. You even owned one once. After the boring compliments there will be time enough to say what is to be said. Then I'll go home, feeling better if not exactly okay, and probably lie at your side. We'll phone the neighbors and have them in.

RAILROADED

Job on the hills . . .
Is that wrong too?
To tell the truth I hardly heard her

what with the wind whistling through the pinecone.
Tell us more about your experience.
That's what really interests our readers.
You know, times when you were down and out

and depressed, like everybody.
When you got up from the table hungry
and didn't eat for a week after that.

Or places with names to which you've fastened a special resonance:
Florence, Florida. Women (and I'm sure there were many)
with whom you spent the night in silken sheets,

or guys (the ones with dicks), I'll wager
there were a few of those too.
Now add salt to the cauldron
of lies and wishes—oversalt,

in fact, or the end result will be downright bland.
I can picture this happening in a kitchen
below some stairs . . .

Darn, I can't help it if there was no room
for my girlfriend's shoes, her vast collection
of pocketbooks with scotties on them.
There never were enough closets,

you see, to go around. We kept things spread out
all over the house. If someone wanted something
he knew where to look for it

and it would probably be there
just as in our time the moon is probably there
where you last looked for it, in one of its phases.

The sun was glorious too
and the marigolds.
Hand me my pickaxe. I think I just overstayed my welcome.
An alarm just went off, some place deep inside.
The wallpaper of my bedroom has been destroyed.
No more angelfish for a while, at least. Too bad.

HONORED GUEST

Accept these nice things we have no use for:
polished twilight, mix of clouds and sun,
minnows in a stream. There may come a time
we'll need them. They're yours forever,
or another dream leaves you thirsty,
waking. You can't see the table
or the bread. How about a clean, unopened letter
and the smell of toast?

School is closed today—it's thundering.
The calendar has backed up or been reversed
so the days have no least common denominator.
Anyway, it was fun, trying to figure out
who you were, what it was that led you to us.
Was it the smell of camphor? Or an ad
in an out-of-state newspaper, seeking news
of someone who disappeared long ago?
He was in uniform, and leaned against a car,
smiling at a girl who seemed to shade her eyes from him.
Can it be? Candace, was it you? There's no way
she'll look our way again.

What can I tell you? Everything's been locked up
for the night, I couldn't get it for you
if I wanted to. But there must be some way—
it's drizzling, the lamps along the path are weeping,
wanting to show you this tremendous thing,
boxed in forever, always getting closer.

OUR LEADER IS DREAMING

Up there our leader is dreaming again.
Down here, timid streets unfold their agendas;
propose, gingerly, a walk out into the night
to view the night sky. What else
is there, you might say, and you'd be right.
Still, someone must be calling the shots. I can hear them
from afar, tapping out some name
in Morse code, making pigeons blink.

Today is still open. I think I'll take some time off,
try to smash this losing streak, until—

It's our founder. He wants to know why you didn't disconnect
his spelling. I said you were off shooting mugwumps
as each emerged, tentatively, from the booby hatch
and hustled back in. Right, but he says you've
let your tennis game go to hell, and he still can't spell
the words the sky proposes to him. Your shelter
isn't taking calls, he says. Instead a curious epiphany
pilots us back to the shoals where a lone telephone booth was last sighted
amid shark-infested eddies. Sparrows are OK,
though, no one wants to kill or eat them. Same goes for carrot tops.
Tell him we've a few gross of those left, too. As for ammunition,
you can't have fuel *and* ammunition. You can have soup, or shoes.

So it was that I departed the caldera, leaving my oboe behind
as security. Its sweet voice haunts me still.
I think I brought you the bloom this time,
will let you know after the last guests have gone. The clouds vanished,
and my headache miraculously thinned,
as on the milk train to Thuringia Falls. To think we could have
once trusted each other, but it's all the same to me. I love me,
and you anyhow.

So the great brazen hump saw us, gazed out over the landscape.

LAST LEGS

My nephew—you remember him—
tongue along a dusty fence.
And I the day's coordinates.
That's what an impression I am.

He was slow to back into the sea,
which ran to meet him, pushing him
on to dry land. Dry land was his place,
after all. He lives there to this day,
with all the hammocks, gramophones,
double old-fashioned glasses, macaques
and expired magazine subscriptions that constitute
a life for some. His framed diploma
from some Methodist medical school,
from which his name is mysteriously absent.
The gold seals are impressive.

By land or sea or foam
I'll get there someday, though—
a particular slice of the past
whose perfume intoxicates, imbibes me
and nobody notices. The sled I was going to take
only it wouldn't fit in my footlocker.
Besides, the tramp steamer was heading for Bahia
or some such.

LEMURS AND PHARISEES

And of course one does run on too long,
but whose fault is it? At five dollars
a blip, who's counting? One could, I suppose,
relax one's discourse, not enough
to frighten it, but to have something cold
in the hand, to cool the palm; the words might
then unspool in a different mode, shadow
of an intention behind the screen
before the lights go up and the generals
sidle on for another confab. "It was *you*
who got us involved in this Dreyfus business." "Liar!"
Let's take a commercial break here,
my head is cobwebby from all the facts
that got stuffed into it this afternoon.

In no way am I the island I was yesterday.
Children and small pets rejoice around my ankles;
yellow ribbons come down from the tree trunks.
This is *my* day! Anybody doesn't realize it
is a goddam chameleon or a yes man! Yes, sir,
we'd noticed your singular pallor, singular
even for you. Ambulances have been summoned,
are rumbling across the delta at this moment,
I'd wager. Meanwhile, if there's anything we can do
to make you comfortable for two or three minutes . . .

The heath is ablaze again. Our longest hose
won't come to within four miles of it.
Don't you realize what this means for us,
for our families, our ancestors? The page,
summoned, duly arrived with the wilted asters
someone had mistakenly ordered. It's a variation
on our habitual not-being-able-to-keep-a-straight-face withdrawal,
turning our back on the smoke and blood-red fumes

we already knew were there, plunging out of hedgerows
so dense not even a titmouse could get through.
Never were we to be invited back again, I mean
no one asked me back again. The others sinned too, each
in her different way, and I have the photographs to prove it,
faded to the ultima thule of legibility.
Next time, you write this.

THE UNDERWRITERS

Sir Joshua Lipton drank this tea
and liked it well enough to start selling it
to a few buddies, from the deck of his yacht.

It spread around the world, became a global
kind of thing. Today everybody knows its story,
and we must be careful not to offend our sponsors,
to humor their slightest whims, no matter how insane
they may seem to us at the time. Like the time one of them
wanted all the infants in the burg aged five or under
to be brought before him, wearing rose-colored sashes,
in order that he might read the Book of Job to them all day.
There were, as you may imagine, many tears shed,
flowing and flopping about, but in the end the old geezer
(the sponsor, not Job) was satisfied, and sank into a sleep more delicate
than any the world had ever known. You see what it's like here—
it's a madhouse, Sir, and I am planning to flee the first time
an occasion presents himself, say as a bag of laundry,
or the cargo of a muffin truck. Meanwhile, the "sands"
of time, as they call them, are slipping by with scarcely a whisper
except for the most lynx-eyed among us. We'll make do,

another day, shopping and such, bringing the meat home at night
all roseate and gleaming, ready for the frying pan.
Our names will be read off a rollcall we won't hear—
how could we? We're not even born yet—the stars will perform their dance
privately, for us, and the pictures in the great black book
that opens at night will enchant us with their yellow harmonies.
We'll manage to get back, someday, to the tie siding where the idea
of all this began, frustrated and a little hungry, but eager
to hear each others' tales of what went on in the interim
of our long lives, what the tea leaves said
and whether it turned out that way. I'll brush your bangs
a little, you'll lean against my hip for comfort.

PALE SIBLINGS

Cheerio. Nothing on the shore
today. Far out to sea, some eczema
mimicking sunlight and shadow, with but temporary success.

Was it for wandering that I have been punished?
Or was it another plot of the siblings,
always anxious to torment, to twist my hair
into witches' brooms, with no inherent power?

Remember they love you like powder
in the air, and it wouldn't take them long at all.
Twenty-five years ago it was different. Please
be patient. Your term too will arrive.

See, he's a very good friend for you, you know that.
You just don't want to sit in a pile of ashes all day long,
licking the milk from your chin. Do you? Then get up
off your ass, stride into the melting twilight,
see the sights of the city. More grass
there than you'd expected, you can bet.

So I wandered fleecy as a cloud and one day an old shepherd crossed my
path, looking very wise with his crook. How much use do you get out of that
thing, I asked him. Depends, he replied. Sometimes one of 'em doesn't go
astray for months on end. Other times I've got my hands full with them run-
ning around in all directions, laughing at me. *At me!* Well, I never would
have taken on this job, this added responsibility, rather, if being thanked
was all I'd had on my mind. Yes, I said, but how do you avoid it when some-
one's really grateful, and graceful, and you're fading away like you're doing
now, your rainbow cap a cigar-store Indian's wooden feather headdress, and
all your daughters frantic with glee or misapprehension as you slide by,
close to them though they can't see you? Oh, I've learned to cope shall we
say, and leave it at that. Yes, I said, by all means, let's.

NOBODY IS GOING ANYWHERE

I don't really understand why you object
to any of this. Personally I am above suspicion.
I live in a crawlup where the mice are rotted,
where midnight tunes absolve the bricklayers
and the ceiling abounds in God's sense.

Something more three-dimensional must be breathed
into action. But go slow, the falling threads
speak to life only as through a haze of difficulty.
The porch is loaded, a question-mark
swings like an earring at the base of your cheek:
stubborn, anxious plain. Air and ice,
those unrelenting fatheads, seem always to be saying,
"This is where we will be living from now on."

In the courtyard a plane tree glistens.

The ship is already far from here, like a ghost ship.
The core of the sermon is always distance, landscape
waiting to be considered, maybe loved a little
eventually. And I do, I do.

POEM ON SEVERAL OCCASIONS

In truth there is room for disquiet
in the wake of the admonitory hiss that accompanies
me wherever I go, to the dentist and back
or sometimes a squeak of approval
will eavesdrop on what I just said,
or even a tiny quiver of applause
will blur in the middle distance, causing
even more distant dogs to bark.

I like to watch the stars giggle and nibble
my hand as I hold it out in a trusting gesture,
like Goethe indicating some Italian hills his companions
might otherwise have overlooked. "I tell you,

it's all in the seasons, or the seasoning, Wolfgang—
otherwise all your inventions might as well have
washed up on a distant strand." That's right,
blame *me* for the ethics issue. Meanwhile can't you
see that children, young adolescents really, are waking
under apple trees, picking up their bookbags listlessly
and traipsing down the road that presumably leads to school?
There they'll read about what we—you and I—have said
to each other on important occasions.

No one will be any wiser. Twenty scarlet nuns
came in and led them off in the direction
of the forest, whence issues a medley of big-band
tunes by forgotten composers from the turn of the century.
Now another century is turning. Will it be pretty or depressed?
What have you to say for that jacket you're wearing, those baggy
pants the color of scarlet elm-leaves?

It will turn out to be a popular color in the new century.
They will call it "white."

SLUMBERER

        Bug-eyed at the possibilities
she slumbers.
I mean there were more of us on anthrax
than not.

        Out of the coal bin
lumbers
our governor. He hasn't been getting too much sleep of late.
Something puzzles him. I know—it's the seepage
of ink in the dairy trough. It bothers him, I now know.

Our way,
that way and in.

Besides, it's elsewhere.
Adventurous.
Wind your way to
the floor.

Noggins were getting a workout,
and all we wanted was the way to the zoo.
We wanted to free the flamingos
but they took off and flew right over our heads,
almost grazing them.
I thought I was going to get knocked down.
Then a kind zoo attendant came over. "It's natural,"
he explained, "at your age (cough, cough), to want to do something
for these pests, or pets, but it's really better to do nothing
for them or anybody. See, they're used to a certain profundity
and get all riled when it's disturbed
even by a well-intentioned impulse such as yours, *especially*
if it's well intentioned. Such, I fear,
is the essence of the tragi-comic. But who could live without it?"

You may well ask, you
who have never done a lick of work save clang metal gates in people's
    pusses.
Point taken, though. We live in an old soup of the tragi-comic.
Werewolves circle us, wishing they were us.
We, on the other hand, wish only that we were somewhere else.
Now are you going to let us into the cage, or what?

Swiftly it was done. A swarm of passenger pigeons whooshed past,
some of them dropping like mayflies, for they were after all extinct,
only some of them hadn't heard about it yet. Other rarae aves
were nowhere to be seen, though the label on the cage
indicated otherwise. But it was old and rusted,
like the cage itself. Hey, does anybody take care of this place?
It's like a ghost-zoo.

Aye, and so it is, my son.
You've only just noticed? Well, we come up with some pretty
extraordinary things down this way—smouldering peat-bog golf courses
with skeleton golfers, hoping for that hole in one
that comes all too regularly.

We have academies for the undistinguished
with long waiting lists, and subscriptions to the opera,
only you wouldn't want to hear any of 'em, not if I was you.
Our pre-schoolers are famished, and the grade school is full of microbes.
I could carry you on my back,
I suppose, across the smouldering turf to the nineteenth hole
where we could wet whistles with some sake and dim sum,
only I wouldn't advise you to stay around much after sunset.
Oh, not that anything funny goes on. Nothing ever does,
in fact. It's just a wide, loose kind of feeling
that refocuses you on yourself like a truant lens

in some aged Kodak, and you see all you can or ever wanted to be,
laid out on the gravel littoral, drying in the sun,
as if there wasn't enough to stink up the place as it is.

Well, I'll be paying my respects to your missus,
who, no offense, knows me better than she may have let on.
But who cares? Life is a carnival,
I think. Besides, it's elsewhere.

Night started to shrivel as he departed.
We were wondering what on earth we were doing here, and how
to extricate ourselves, should we ever really want to.

POT LUCK

You always leave me where we left off.
You bring me every little thing,
which is probably a mistake.
You shaved my canary once.
I am anxious to be out by the speedway.
At least, almost nothing happens there.
I was drugged by a cat once
on the edge of Lake Lucerne. Woke
feeling like a businessman without portfolio.
Wait, here goes a new one. He'll examine the fork
to see if it's rooted. Well, it is. In danger.
In the past, which is much the same thing.

So we dance the bolero in times like these.
I believe I am slimmer than my last bathing suit.
Tommy sat on the step, looking so cute. It was
run for your lives, now or never. Now
I don't feel so much better. I had dropped off the letter
at the office, thinking it would be quicker.
Perhaps the editor never got it. I enjoy playing
the glass harmonica, am slender and look half my age.
Catcher in the Rye is my all-time favorite book.

And how about you? Do you, too, come out here
with your family on Saturday afternoons, hoping
for a little rest and relaxation, far
from the city and its desks? Here they have daffodils.
Look, there is one over there by the city.
They have a name for it. "Detroit."

And all the time I thought I was being a pest
someone was desperately in love with me.
The person sickened and apparently died
in a hospital far away. Now I have no one,

no friends to gripe with or call coaxing names to.
I was definitely born at the wrong time
or in the wrong city. Pot-luck dinners were shared.
I thought I had gone to hell. Too bad I woke up in time.

SHORT-TERM MEMORY

A few things came to observe me:
a terrible explosion,
flowers, dustiness in the boroughs,
planners plagued by increasingly goofy proposals.

I could have pretended not to be in.
Instead I came to the door in shirtsleeves,
extending a hand to the vexed guests. "What about those Orioles,
this terribly warm weather we've been having?" Truthfully,
I was suffering from the heat and didn't know it.
It was enough just then to perceive life as a sandbar,
or a mirage of one, that the tide is frantically
trying to erase so as to cover its tracks.

Broken discoveries invaded my short-term memory,
but not so you'd notice. Continuing the polite
palaver I asked after the health of this one and that one,
how little Lois was doing in school, what Howie was up to
in his treehouse. It was as though no one cared.
Or had seen me. They shuffled aimlessly away
to come alive later no doubt in some sex sequence,
while here leaves are browning before the end of summer
and the groundskeeper waits.

What about your immortal soul?
I may have lost it, just this once, but other chapters
will arrive, bright as a child's watercolor,
and you'd want to be around me.

VENDANGES

A tall building in the fifteenth arrondissement faded away slowly and then completely vanished. Toward November the weather grew very bitter. No one knew why or even noticed. I forgot to tell you your hat looked perky.

A new way of falling asleep has been discovered. Senior citizens snoop around to impose that sleep. You awake feeling refreshed but something has changed. Perhaps it's the children singing too much. Sophie shouldn't have taken them to the concert. I pleaded with her at the time, to no avail. Also, they have the run of the yard. Someone else might want to use it, or have it be empty. All the chairs were sat on in one night.

And I was pale and restless. The actors walked with me to the cabins. I knew that someone was about to lose or destroy my life's work, or invention. Yet something urged calm on me.

There is an occasional friend left, yes. Married men, hand to mouth. I went down to the exhibition. We came back and listened to some records. Strange, I hadn't noticed the lava pouring. But it's there, she said, every night of the year, like a river. I guess I notice things less now than I used to,

when I was young.

And the arbitrariness of so much of it, like sheep's wool from a carding comb. You can't afford to be vigilant, she said. You must stay this way, always, open and vulnerable. Like a body cavity. Then if you are noticed it will be too late to file the architectural pants. We must, as you say, keep in touch. Not to be noticed. If it was for this I was born, I murmured under my breath. What have I been doing around here, all this month? Waiting for the repairman, I suppose.

Where were you when the last droplets dribbled? Fastening my garter belt to my panty hose. The whole thing was over in less time than you could say Jack Robinson and we were back at base camp, one little thing after another gone wrong, yet on the whole life is spiritual. Still, it is time to pull up stakes. Probably we'll meet a hooded stranger on the path who will point out a direction for us to take, and that will be okay too, interesting even if it's boring.

I remember the world of cherry blossoms looking up at the sun and wondering, what have I done to deserve this or anything else?

SMALL CITY

Small city where I lived for some years in total darkness,
whose pale terminology took over
my varied instincts for right and wrong.
Sometimes in the long evenings one would stop talking,
then, if the topic was, say, shoes
the others would mouth their assent. I cannot go in or out
of doors to this day without recalling your vocabulary
of dirty words that no longer count. I mean they are clean now.
The working dead pitch in at seven.

A new table had taken your hands.
You should move into it, dining space,
letting the wine of your spit wander over and muzzle
the hollow square of guards out in the square.
One was always missing, or so it seemed,
but they had ingenious ways of disguising it,
like a pretty girl in a shawl was sent to the doctor's
to reclaim some suds, and nobody noticed her by the
time we'd realized she was gone. The antlers over the vitrine
however grew clammy and trembled—
no doubt at the thought of some sport
infinitely postponed, or curtailed.
Yet we followed where her eyes led dancing, wild topic.
Find hordes! Or else it was all over in the suburbs
whose furious light beat like an ornery orrery.
The band marched in and played the doctor symphony
while we were talking amongst ourselves. What to do next?
There was bread in the breadbox
but all the shoe stores were closed.

We like our pixillated selves
in that tertiary period, yet always
a vague dissatisfaction gnawed at our tripes.
There was mewing between the thunderclaps.

We were sure we wouldn't get out alive,
yet we always did, somehow. Someone must have told on us, though,
for we were made to stand in the basement
as the hours oozed through the window grill.
We knew we could catch up
someday when foam would caress the weir
and black-eyed susans stumbled.

It is not a happy place to be
until after the rain has ended.

VINTAGE MASQUERADE

That article I'd meant to read—
you saw it first, a while ago, in some magazine,
perused it and forgot its major tenets.
Only the ghost of its prose rhythms served you,
like water at the base of a log
some minnow undermines.

So they never came for us in the suburbs
of what city we were living in at that time.
We lived undisturbed, in the manner of the great dead writers:
metallic coffee in the morning, then work until almost noon
with a couple of poached eggs on rye toast then, then more
of the same till afternoon shadows lengthened, and it was time
to go for a long walk and play ambush. Stealthily we'd return,
sampling the largesse of unknown ancestors,
admiring the way those rocks look on business trips,
blush that suffuses the whole earth. Tell me,
can you remember any of this? I, who put it all down,
I cannot, and so let the living choose my books
at the rental library, evening's salad from the greengrocer's.

If there is more to remember, I gift you with it
because of the eternal person you were sometimes, and the loveliness
of your being, shaken clear of you like duck feathers.

TO GOOD PEOPLE WHO SHOULD BE GOING
SOMEWHERE ELSE

Apricots: "Oh, there won't be any again this year."
—Flaubert, *Dictionary of Received Ideas*

Many couldn't stop being in love with you,
and that in a decade. In the pileup every noble
impulse is disgraced, every overture rebuffed,
no matter how insincere. A wall of plums towers
over the effort at tilling. Usually they paint it up
so you can see it in the haze. Not today.

A freckled girl misunderstands me and laughs,
as though I were part of her explanation.
"You see, the boys drive right through you.
And I thought *I* was invisible." Hon, it's your hat,
not your fault, that evening headlines tilt at.
Everywhere is a great fuss, though there were parishes
of tranquillity only last week. They decided to change things
just because things ought to change, or else because they do, anyway.
Peace in the distance is merely a metallic whine,
the fruit concurs. And now very seldom.

ANOTHER AARDVARK

I cannot recommend your curls too highly—
that is, I cannot recommend them. Sometimes
I wish I could, whenas in silks
you go, past the cat's dish
and on into the living room. I wish
there was some way to add a story-line, or patter,
melody, whatever you want to call it,
but there just isn't. Something greater
than us approaches, calls down to us:
Has he left the building? Is the theater empty,
really empty, its rows of red velvet seats
devoid of a single guest, or ghost?

There was a party last night but I didn't go,
couldn't stand the ruckus, the questions
people put to you: How do you like living
in your new house? Fine. I moved there twenty-five
years ago, but it all still seems new to me,
the sink especially. Then you spend a lot of time
in the bathroom? No, it was my books I was talking about,
my treasured library. I don't see how anyone can read
too many books, do you? Am I delusional? Is it a forest
that's approaching, with its format of shadows,
wind among its grasses? And all this time
I thought you were asleep. I took a long walk.
Ended up next door. Ed had been hitting the sneaky pete
again. And I have things to do, walks to shovel,
before the next train, and the grain
that is sure to follow in its wake.

HAS TO BE SOMEWHERE

Having escaped the first box,
I wandered into a fenced-off arena
from which the distance, peach-blue, could be ascertained:

convenient for my adventures
at this period of my life. Yet I wriggled farther into an indeterminate space
that was actually a mood, or many moods, one overlaying another
like gift wrap.

This is actually what was supposed to take place:
a duet of duelling cuckoos, at the close of which the winner
gets to stand next to me for the photo-op.

Alas, things went terribly wrong.
For I can now claim no space as rightfully mine
and must stand at the edge of the crowd like a ghost
for an unforeseeable length of time.

All this because I meant to be polite to someone.
We had met in the desert, you see, and he wished for a warm place
that wasn't the desert, and I said, "Why not try my hometown?
It's warm in winter. Sometimes."

Days later at the hotel bar I learned his real name
and his reason for wanting to trail me to my so-called hometown,
where I had never felt at home, yet never dreamed
of wishing for another. He said our great-great-grandmothers had been
    friends
in France, in the time of Marie de Médicis. "In any case
you can't let me down now, now that I've tracked you here
and seen how you actually live."

Was that meant to be a compliment? I suppose not,
yet something in his bright-eyed delivery made me imagine

I'd found a new long-lost friend. "Let's go visit the post office,"
I proposed, and he eagerly assented. Walking the narrow streets
I would never again recognize, I got this wistful feeling,
like a long, slow song sung from the tip of a distant tower.
I'd been rejected again, yet how? Nothing had really happened.
My friend was looking straight ahead, not saying anything.

"Is this the place you wanted to come to?
It's not much, I know. Terrazzo floor, frosted panes, a bit of brass
handle here and there, like a handle on a bedpost."

"What's that supposed to mean," he said, and sighed.
"Tomorrow I must be in Ottawa.
I'd hoped to spend the whole day with you, but now it's getting dark
and my bus will be leaving shortly." How could he do this to me?
Easily enough, apparently. "But what about Marie de Médicis?"
I stammered, as the mist broke and then reformed its ranks.
"Shucks, there's not much you can do in Ottawa on a Tuesday."
"That's what you think," came the curt reply. Now all is darkness.

THE DON'S BEQUEST

It's often more crazy like this
as I slide the wooden greyhounds along
their respective slots, ever in pursuit of the elusive hare
or is it a note of music, a particularly silvery one
heard only once, in the bow of a ship
what seems like ages ago?

In any case they are
dispiritingly spirited in quest of the elusive eidolon,
waft of breeze—was that laughter?—trimmed wick, whatever.
And we all know the race ends soon,
soon enough to be over.

So I spray this collection of days and hours
from the fat old album with a mist of Florida water,
something to bring them down
and to their senses simultaneously.
That's all I get for my pains—a glimpse
of beard through the judas peephole as it slides back,
then shut. The barren February street still assumes
a fleeting charm, known only to itself.
At least I never met anybody who was familiar with it,
knew its surname.

It's time to make my bequest to the land
we all landed on, and will be leaving at some point
in a hot-air balloon painted voluminous colors. I said
we could keep some of the currants, you didn't have to hog the whole
     bushel.
And so it goes, earth crunching underfoot,
interesting thoughts flowing through the head, the scalp in heaven.
When I see a cabinful of these wanderers I want to shout, though.
Why can't you all go back to chafing and wondering?
Yes, that's what we all do best.

STRANGE CINEMA

In sooth, I come here sadly,
not trembling, not against my will,
hoping you will set the record straight.
You can, you know, in a minute
if the wind is right and no felon intervenes.

And we sit and you tell me how crazy I am.
I shall petition the other board members
but am afraid nothing will ever come right.
It has been going on too long for this to happen,
yet it was right to go, to go on as it did,
even if there was a strangeness in the rightness
that no one can now see. They see the night
in its undress, plaits unplaited, brushed,
the sound of the surf churning on distant rocks,
can think only about how heavenly it would have been
if it had all happened later or differently.

Now, according to some sources,
new retrofitting trends are a commodity,
along with silence, and sweetness.
Doucement, doucement . . .

And when the sweetness is adjusted,
why, we'll know more than some do now.
That is all I can offer you,
my lost, my loved one.

A STAR BELCHED

On she danced, but had forgotten
how fancy it all was, how plain too.
Outside the silver motel they greeted her:
"Lotta traffic today." But she made no semblant
of hearing. "I say, he's big sir."
And on and on. The basement held no magic for her

nor for us anymore. It was as though we had come home
to dine on a single lamb chop, and it was gone.
The rain peered in the window
and directed its gaze succinctly at the linoleum.
All passion had been drained from the deep.
They might as well write it on blackboards.
Yet I was having too good a time to stop thinking yet.

Overhead the manager rushed. Now don't pull
my sweater away like that. Yet in time manure produces cherries
the clerk murmured. So we all forgot to compare these groans
to the ones suffering had caused, back in the vengeful night.
The moment I stare I kiss you.

WHEN PRESSED

Why has the sailor come in
too late? What star waters the garden?

You do intelligent things
at the first juxtaposition.
Luck is the composite of all these forces.
By then experience itself has been outlasted.
The grass shrivels.

It seems they came to lunch, through mist, on a Sunday many years ago.
On a sandwich plate was a letter, written in ivy,
casting doubt on the bearer,
your great-uncle.

They lingered, and fell apart.
We grew up impeccably, caught in the vise of sleep,
frequently taken advantage of.

Return me to that sense which I don't know.
Encased in a world, not seeing anything wrong
with how it grew, not getting better.
The juxtaposition happens again, farther along this time with a rueful
     elegance.
The painters have whitewashed the building,
our roof looks sleepy. And they, the witnesses inside,
they had heard something of this.

We keep on extricating, not certain the patch is over
or what it included up till now.
Is someone slap-happy? Are all parades uncertain, rinsed
of cloud, like a tree in a tear.
Note that the box has been "discontinued."

THE IMPURE

Your story . . . most enjoyable.
I sat down and read it through from
beginning to end at one sitting,
whatever it is. Reams and reams of it.

White ambulances chase each other through the mist
and the fish swim by, too haughty
to have an opinion on anything.

These timed-release capsules work very well
but how could anyone know that? We are where
we began. This gray October day

that no one could have imagined, save Mama and Papa
sitting on their porch, having doubts about the weather.
When they go inside
it will all be over.

Casting about for some impurities
in your rock-crystal speech, I was struck by a tone
only mute dragonflies can keep up for long.

Then I thought about your brother Ben,
gone so long in the far land.
Would he return with the car,
with garlands flowing from its fenders,
to utter the word "drizzle"? Oh, Ben,
we liked you so much for such a long time.
Then you became insufferable to us
in just a few moments, for no reason. And now
we think we like you, Ben.

CROWD CONDITIONS

Across the frontier, imperfect sympathies are twinkling,
a petite suite of lights in the gaga sky.
Most of the important things had to be obliterated
for this to happen. Does that interest you, *ma jolie?*
Something else would have happened in any case,
more to your liking, perhaps. Yet we can't undo the sexual posture
that comes with everything, a free gift.

Now the blades are shifting in the forest.
The ocean sighs, finding the process of striking the shore
interminable and intolerable. Let's pretend it's back when we were young
and cheap, and nobody followed us. Well,
that's not entirely true: The poodle followed us
home from school sometimes. Men in limousines followed us
at a discreet distance, the back seat banked with roses.
But as we got older one couldn't take a step
without creating crowd conditions. Men dressed like reporters
in coats and hats with visors, and yes, old ladies too,
crooning about the loss they supposed we shared with them.

Forget it. It all comes undone sooner or later.
The vetch goes on growing, wondering
whether it grew any more today.
Such, my friends, is life, wondered the president.

ENJOYS WATCHING FOREIGN FILMS

To stay here forever. To lie down.
Lord, let us leave these petty shacks
of masonite, this angular scrub-forest,
speaking incessantly of the love of man
for woman, of woman for man, of man
for man, of woman for both woman and man,
and journey to some antique pergola
whose orange lozenges cast the light of reason
on these appalled, formal faces.

And if we size up all that
crushed fabric that lies across the river,
pretending to no dream, no appetite, why then I
will become the accuser of the race in myself. I cannot outrun
the gibbets at the New York City limits,
but perhaps things are better off this way.
You can see clear into the checkered chevrons
of a child's eyes, thirsting for grace
with the other millions. O don't give up, just
pretend it's Monopoly we're playing,
and I've just landed in your hotel.

FADE IN

Continually detouring among the mountains,
some got lost, bathed in freshets.
Others stumbled onto the fringes of a large city
just as revolt was breaking out. Tourists, they were told,
should not try to escape, but enjoy the genuine hospitality
of the country, its superior hotels, some with rooms facing the ocean,
all provided with the latest in fitness equipment.
"Sure, try to put a good face on it, make nice with the natives
staring at us. I wonder when the bars open, or if they do."

Back at the Hotel Frisson the mood was one
of subdued reproach, such as a tardy guest feels, even
after apologies have been made and accepted.
Metallic fronds brushed against the catwalks.
Every so often a child would come, always silent,
with simple gifts in her hands, like a rabbit eraser.

This couldn't quite compare with real life though,
as we thought we had experienced it in the past,
even the very recent past. The monsoon, striking at five,
just as elaborate drinks were at last being served,
canceled civility, forcing huge residents to flee.

OVER AT THE MUTTS'

Funny, it says "hidden drive." *Look where you're going!*
I do, yet no drive emerges. Later on, maybe.

Tune in next week. My midair flight: live, awkward being.
Like the console radio says, none too consolingly,
you are your own hair and father.

Don't ever live close to a canal. The noise of fish
is ear-splitting. When the barometer plunges it takes you with it.
I don't mind heat so much, though.
It's the barometric pressure against my zinc-lined stomach
that makes me come on all funny. Hey, can I come over?

She's gone and stitched the lining to his dinner pail
filled it with nail polish remover
and left for the station. Next train isn't till forty-eight hours
from now. That's all right, I'll wait. Where does it go?
Oh, lots of places that have plums and wolverines in them,
but it's the jacket of your report card that interests me now.
Let me see it.

Why is it they always run out of party favors?
Here, I'll look for some more, on the ground.
The forest wind-chimes are favorable tonight
and the horehound drops toothsome.

She was dancing in the next part of her living.
Yes, she danced, and it didn't matter to her,
though others admired her gaze, her step, her hair's moist highlights.

I brought you over to make something out of myself.
I'm sorry. I should have left you at home, between the bookends.
Oh, but it's all right! Really! This afterlife has been a learning experience.
I am gradually turning to chalk, taking both of us with them,
and it'll be all right in the morning too. I guarantee it.

PASTILLES FOR THE VOYAGE

If it is spring it matters a little,
or not. Some are running down
to get into their cars, shoving
old ladies out of the way. I say,
dude, it made more sense a while ago
when we was on the grass. Tell it to the Ages,
that's what they're there for. You know,
miscellaneous record-keeping, and the like,
the starving of fools
and transformation of opera singers
into the characters they're supposed to be onstage.
Here comes Tosca, chattering with Isolde
about some vivacious bird's egg winter left behind.

I turn the corner into my street
and see them all, all the things that have mattered
to me during my long life: the dung-beetle
who was convinced he could tap dance; the grocer's boy
(he hasn't changed much in eighty years, nor have I);
and the amorphous crowd in black T-shirts with names like
slumlords or slumgullion spattered over them. O my friends
(for I have no other), the beginning of fermentation is *here*,
right on this sidewalk or whatever you call it.
We know, they say, and keep going.
If only I could get the tears out of my eyes it would be raining now.
I must try the new, fluid approach.

OF THE LIGHT

That watery light, so undervalued
except when evaluated, which never happens
much, perhaps even not at all—I intend to conserve it
somehow, in a book, in a dish, even at night,
like an insect in a light bulb.

Yes, day may just be breaking. The importance isn't there
but in the beautiful flights of the trees
accepting their own flaccid destiny,
or the tightrope of seasons.
We get scared when we look at them up close
but the king doesn't mind. He has the tides to worry about,

and how fitting is the new mood of contentment
and how long it will wear thin.

I looked forward to seeing you so much
I have dragged the king from his lair: There,
take that, you old wizard. Wizard enough, he replies,
but this isn't going to save us from the light
of breakfast, or mend the hole in your stocking.
"Now wait"—and yet another day has consumed itself,
brisk with passion and grief, crisp as an illustration in a magazine
from the thirties, when we and this light were all that mattered.

YOUR NAME HERE

But how can I be in this bar and also be a recluse?
The colony of ants was marching toward me, stretching
far into the distance, where they were as small as ants.
Their leader held up a twig as big as a poplar.
It was obviously supposed to be for me.
But he couldn't say it, with a poplar in his mandibles.
Well, let's forget that scene and turn to one in Paris.
Ants are walking down the Champs-Elysées
in the snow, in twos and threes, conversing,
revealing a sociability one never supposed them as having.
The larger ones have almost reached the allegorical statues
of French cities (is it?) on the Place de la Concorde.
"You see, I told you he was going to bolt.
Now he just sits in his attic
ordering copious *plats* from a nearby restaurant
as though God had meant him to be quiet."
"While you are like a portrait of Mme de Staël by Overbeck,
that is to say a little serious and washed out.
Remember you can come to me anytime
with what is bothering you, just don't ask for money.
Day and night my home, my hearth are open to you,
you great big adorable one, you."

The bar was unexpectedly comfortable.
I thought about staying. There was an alarm clock on it.
Patrons were invited to guess the time (the clock was always wrong).
More cheerful citizenry crowded in, singing the Marseillaise,
congratulating each other for the wrong reasons, like the color
of their socks, and taking swigs from a communal jug.
"I just love it when he gets this way,
which happens in the middle of August, when summer is on its way
out, and autumn is still just a glint in its eye,
a chronicle of hoar-frost foretold."
"Yes and he was going to buy all the candy bars in the machine

126

but something happened, the walls caved in (who knew
the river had risen rapidly?) and one by one people were swept away
calling endearing things to each other, using pet names.
'Achilles, meet Angus.' " Then it all happened so quickly I
guess I never knew where we were going, where the pavement
was taking us.

Things got real quiet in the oubliette.
I was still reading *Jean-Christophe*. I'll never finish the darn thing.
Now is the time for you to go out into the light
and congratulate whoever is left in our city. People who survived
the eclipse. But I was totally taken with you, always have been.
Light a candle in my wreath, I'll be yours forever and will kiss you.